WHAT'S UP?

American Idioms

Pamela McPartland

Hunter College
City University of New York

Photographs by Anne Turyn

PRENTICE HALL REGENTS

To the memory of my father,
Laurence McPartland

Library of Congress Cataloging-in-Publication Data

McPartland, Pamela.
  What's up?

  1. Americanisms.   2. English language—United
States—Idioms.   3. English language—Textbooks for
foreign speakers.   I. Title.
PE2827.M25 1989   428′.00973   88–32385
ISBN 0-13-955766-0

Editorial/production supervision: Janet S. Johnston
Manufacturing buyers: Laura Crossland, Mike Woerner
Photographs: Anne Turyn
Cover design: Wanda Lubelska Design

©1989 by Prentice Hall Regents

Printed in the United States of America

20 19 18 17 16

ISBN 0-13-955766-0

CONTENTS

ACKNOWLEDGMENTS

Several people helped me with this book. First, I'd like to thank all the teachers and students who used *Take It Easy* and encouraged me to write another book on idioms.

The anonymous reviewers for Prentice Hall Regents were inspirational in their rigorous approach to the review process.

I am indebted to Susan Stempleski, Alison Rice, and Julie Falsetti, my colleagues at the International English Language Institute, for the models of communicative activities they developed in their book *Getting Together*. I would also like to acknowledge Gertrude Moskowitz's classic work, *Caring and Sharing in the Foreign Language Classroom*, as a fine reference for interactive activities.

For cheerfully field testing *What's Up?* when it wasn't fit to print and for sharing students' writing with me, I thank Kathryn Nikodem, another colleague at the Institute.

Victoria Henriquez turned very rough drafts into neatly typed pages and stayed with the project through multiple drafts. Joan Quintana cheerfully typed the final changes, under pressure, before publication.

Two ESL students at the Institute, Tony Piccolo and Enrique Ortiga, drew my attention to the idiom "What's up?" which led to my choosing it as the title of this book.

My sister, Mary Ann McPartland, edited the reading selections, and Brenda White, my editor at Prentice Hall Regents, provided the right combination of patience and pressure to help me finish the book. Janet Johnston and Louisa Hellegers meticulously copyedited the manuscript.

Finally, I'd like to thank my friend Betsy Baiker for her constant encouragement and regular supply of comics while I was simultaneously writing this book and a doctoral dissertation.

TO THE STUDENT

What's Up? is a book about idioms. In fact, "What's up?" is an idiom. An idiom is a group of words that has a special meaning. The meaning of the group of words is different from the meanings of the individual words together. For example, the group of words "What's up?" means "What's new?" or "What's happening?" The word "up" alone does not mean "new" or "happening," but when it's combined with "what's," it means "What's new?"

This doesn't mean that every group of words is an idiom. For example, "up the hill" is a group of words, but it doesn't have a special meaning. Each word has its ordinary meaning. In this example, "up" means the opposite of "down."

Many of the words used in idioms come from Old English or Middle English, ancestors of the English we use today. Their one-word equivalents often come from Latin or Greek. For example, the Old English words "turn down" mean "reject," a Latin word. Because so many of the words used in idioms are English in origin (not Latin or Greek), idioms are at the heart of the English language.

Although idioms often sound less formal than their one-word equivalents, this doesn't mean that idioms are slang or incorrect forms of English. Most idioms are standard forms of expression and are used in literature, magazine and newspaper articles, academic journals, speeches, and radio and television broadcasts, as well as in everyday speech.

By doing the exercises in this book, you will learn to understand and use seventy-three idioms. You will practice using idioms in reading, writing, speaking, and listening. You will not only learn the meaning of each idiom, you will also learn:

1. the subjects and objects that go with the idiom. For example, "Judy called up her sister."
2. the words in the idiom that are stressed. For example, in "work on" only "work" is stressed, but in "work out" both words are stressed.

3. the position of pronoun objects. For example, you can say: "Judy called up her sister," or you can say: "Judy called her sister up." But if you use a pronoun, you must say: "Judy called her up." You can't say: "Judy called up her" unless you are contrasting "her" with someone else.

4. if the idiom is informal. For example, "polish off": "Victor polished off a hamburger and a soda in about one minute."

By doing the exercises and activities in *What's Up?* you will get a lot of practice with idioms in sentences, paragraphs, and stories. You will read sentences with idioms in them, write sentences with idioms, hear sentences with idioms, and say sentences with idioms. After you finish each chapter, you will have a good idea of how to use the idioms introduced in that chapter.

Of course, you won't know all the idioms in English (there are thousands of them), but you will know many idioms, and you will know how to learn more on your own. And the next time someone asks you "What's up?," you can tell that person: "I've been studying English idioms, and 'What's up?' is one of them!"

TO THE TEACHER

What's Up? is a book of verbal idioms. Each chapter presents five to ten idioms related to a specific topic (such as family, sports, politics, and lifestyles) in a meaningful context, with follow-up exercises and activities to help learners develop syntactic and communicative competence in this important aspect of the English lexicon. The book contains ten chapters and two review sections.

The material is geared to **intermediate** ESL or EFL learners. The idioms are presented in reading selections about contemporary topics (such as illiteracy, dieting, and famous authors). The contexts appeal to both adult and young-adult learners.

What's Up? uses an inductive approach to the study of idioms. Learners read a story containing a number of idioms and then answer **comprehension, inference,** and **main idea** questions based on the contextualized presentation. Learners again use the context to determine the precise **meaning** of each idiom. But knowing the meaning of an idiom is not enough if a learner wants to develop fluency with idioms. The text therefore provides additional exercises in **selectional restrictions** (that is, the subjects and objects appropriate to each idiom), **prepositions** and **particles,** the **position of object pronouns,** as well as information on the **grammatical** and **stylistic characteristics** of certain idioms and the placement of **stress** in each idiom.

After learners have worked on exercises that draw attention to the **semantic** and **syntactic** properties of the idioms, they go on to exercises and activities that provide **listening comprehension** practice, **writing** practice, and **conversation** practice. In the course of each chapter, learners practice idioms through all four skills: **reading, writing, speaking,** and **listening.** The book does not contain mechanical drills that students can do by simply following a model. Instead, each exercise requires the learner to make hypotheses about the idioms, so the learner is gradually acquiring more and more information about the peculiarities of each idiom. The following is a list of the exercises and activities that appear in each chapter:

Warm-Up Exercise

Reading Exercises (Get the Picture? Comprehension; Get the Picture? Inferences; Get the Picture? Main Idea)

Meaning Exercises (Figure It Out; What Does It Go With?; Look It Up)

Grammar Exercises (Fill It In: Prepositions and Particles; Fill It In: Object Pronouns)

Listening Comprehension Exercise (Listen In)
Writing Exercise (Finish It Up)
Conversation Activities (Act It Out; Talk It Over)

What's Up? can be used for special classes in idioms, vocabulary, listening comprehension or conversation, or as an ancillary text for grammar, reading, or writing courses. Also, this material can be used in T.O.E.F.L. preparation courses because idioms are frequently incorporated in the listening comprehension section of the test, and the book may be used for self-study (an Answer Key is in the Appendix) and in a language lab.

The idioms are presented in reading, writing, speaking, and listening activities because idioms occur in all these aspects of American English. People commonly believe that idioms are limited to spoken English, but idioms are used in literature, newspaper articles, advertisements, business reports, and academic publications.

The idioms selected for this text are, for the most part, idioms that occur frequently. Although some are less formal than others ("go for," "polish off," and "root for," for example, are less formal than "come in contact with," "focus on," and "put into power"), the text contains no slang, because slang tends to become outdated quickly, and its use is limited mainly to informal, spoken English.

BY THE WAY . . .

This text is not meant to be an exhaustive treatment of idioms in English. It deals with verbal idioms exclusively, and only with seventy-three out of the more than 10,000 idioms that exist in the language. The point is not to teach learners to master every idiom in English, but to help them become conscious of idioms and learn how to use some of them. Because transitive phrasal verbs are separable (that is, an object can occur between the verb and particle, such as "The university turned his application for financial aid down"), learners who have not studied idioms aren't aware that the words "turn" and "down" have a special meaning, i.e., to "reject." After working through this text, learners should be able to notice the connections between verbs and particles and verbs and prepositions in the input they get from native speakers, and to continue to learn idioms when the course is over.

ABOUT THE EXERCISES

Warm-Up Exercise

This is loosely connected to the reading passage but is more personal in nature. It gives students a chance to get to know each other, and should lead to a positive classroom atmosphere while introducing students to the theme of the chapter.

Reading Exercises

These exercises are a follow-up to the reading passage through which students are introduced to the idioms of the chapter. Through comprehension, inference, and main idea questions, students learn to make hypotheses about the meaning of the idioms in context.

Meaning Exercises

The *Figure It Out* exercise helps students grasp the precise meaning of each idiom. Each line is part of a story, so the context builds from sentence to sentence. *What Does It Go With?* helps students develop an awareness of which subjects and objects go with each idiom. *Look It Up* allows the student to use some of the information learned earlier in the chapter, and introduces new information, such as where the stress falls in the idiom and what grammatical and stylistic traits characterize that idiom. *Note:* If the reading selection is too difficult for a particular class, start with the meaning exercises and then go to the reading selection and reading exercises.

Grammar Exercises

Fill It In: Prepositions and Particles is an exercise that draws students' attention to the prepositions and particles that co-occur with verbs to form idioms. This exercise is also a story, which provides learners with another example of the idioms in context. This exercise is on the cassette, so students can check their answers by listening to the tape. *Note:* This exercise could also be used as a pretest to determine if the learners know any of the idioms before they work on a chapter. *Fill It In: Object Pronouns* is an exercise that helps learners recognize that the pronoun object goes between the verb and the particle, but after the preposition in the case of a verb-preposition combination. *Note:* This exercise does not include idioms that don't take a pronoun object (some take only a gerund) or any object at all.

Listening Comprehension Exercise

Listen In provides an opportunity for students to hear the idioms presented in new situations in a voice other than the teacher's or other students'. This exercise helps students develop confidence in their ability to understand the precise meaning of spoken utterances.

Writing Exercise

In *Finish It Up*, students complete a diary entry that has been started for them, requiring learners to generate their own sentences with idioms. This exercise gives the learners a chance to demonstrate their knowledge of the meaning of the idioms, the subjects and objects that go with the idioms, the position of pronoun objects, and any particular grammatical or stylistic characteristics of the idioms. When writing, students have time to attend to all of these details and to edit their work. *Note:* The photograph that opens each chapter may be used for additional writing practice.

Conversation Activities

Act It Out helps students create their own sentences with idioms in the contexts provided. For variety, different groups may act out different situations, or groups may want to invent their own settings. *Talk It Over* gets the students out of their chairs to interact with their classmates. The exercise requires comprehension of the idioms and, like the warm-up exercise, encourages students to learn more about each other. Some chapters contain additional *Talk It Over* activities that generate discussion about the theme of the chapter. *Note:* The photograph that opens each chapter may also be used for additional conversation practice.

Review Sections

Review I: Mix Them Up gives learners additional practice with the thirty-one idioms in Chapters 1 through 5. *Review II: What's Up?* brings together all the idioms in Chapters 1 through 10.

What's Up? contains many exercises, and it isn't necessary to do every one in class. Students can work on the multiple-choice exercises at home and do the more communicative exercises (that is, *Warm-Up, Act It Out*, and *Talk It Over*) in class. Of course, if the tape is used, exercises requiring the tape should be done in class (*Fill It In: Prepositions and Particles*, and *Listen In*).

If there isn't sufficient time to cover all the exercises, choose those that are appropriate to the level of the class and the subject matter to be stressed in the course (for example, listening or conversation). If students want to cover all the exercises, they can do them on their own and check their answers in the Answer Key in the appendix. The pages are perforated, so the Answer Key can be removed if it proves to be too much of a temptation during the learning process.

TYPES OF IDIOMS

This book presents four types of verbal idioms:

Idiom	Example
1. verb + particle (also called "phrasal verbs" or "two-word verbs")	bring up, catch on
2. verb + preposition (also called "prepositional verbs")	stick to, become of
3. verb + particle + preposition (also called "three-word verbs")	sign up for, drop out of
4. complex combinations, e.g.: verb + preposition + noun + preposition	get in touch with
verb + article + noun + preposition	make an impression on

Notice that the stress patterns differ. In general, particles (also called "adverbs" or "adverbial particles") are stressed, but prepositions are unstressed unless the preposition has more than one syllable. For example, "turn into" has stress on the first syllable of the preposition "into."

Another difference involves the position of objects. In transitive verb + particle combinations, the noun object can go between the verb and the particle (for example, "bring *the children* up") or after the particle ("bring up *the children*"). But if a pronoun object is used, it must go between the verb and the particle ("bring *them* up"). In all other verbal idioms, the object goes after the preposition, whether it's a noun or a pronoun (for example, "stick to *it*," "sign up for *a course*," "get in touch with *her*," "make an impression on *them*").

By definition, the meaning of an idiom cannot be derived from the individual meanings of its parts. There are varying degrees of idiomaticity, however: from those that are close to literal (such as "win out") to those that are highly idiomatic (such as "break out"). This book contains all types. Some are actually not idiomatic at all, but are included because the words that make up the combination have such a strong tendency to occur together (such as "plan on" and "vote for"). In other words, the selection of idioms in *What's Up?* tends to be more inclusive than exclusive.

WHAT'S UP?

Inset photo © Robert Bindler.

1   SPORTS

WARM-UP EXERCISE

Which sports do you like to watch?

_____

_____

_____

Which sports do you like to participate in?

_____

_____

_____

If you don't like sports, which other activities do you like, for example, dancing, reading?

_____

_____

_____

Share your favorite sports or other activities with the class.

READING SELECTION

DIRECTIONS: Read the following story silently. Then do the reading exercises that follow.

Go for It

Mark Spitz said he would win six gold medals in swimming events[1] at the 1968 Olympic Games in Mexico City. But it wasn't that easy; Spitz was **competing against** some of the best athletes[2] in the world. He won only two gold medals, not six, but those two showed that he **was good at** the sport.

The people who **rooted for** Spitz at the '68 Games saw him again four years later. In the 1972 Olympic Games in Munich, Spitz decided to **go for** the gold once more. Again, he **stood out.** He won not six, but seven, gold medals: three as a member of U.S. teams and four in individual events. This made Mark Spitz the first athlete to win seven gold medals at the same Games.

What is the five-ounce medal worth? The "gold" medal is really 92 percent silver, so it is not worth very much money. But because of his Olympic success, Spitz appeared in many television commercials, so his gold medals were worth several million dollars.

1. Contests in a program.
2. People trained in sports requiring strength, skill, and speed.

I. READING EXERCISES

A. Get the Picture? Comprehension

DIRECTIONS: These questions are based on the story you just read. Write "True" or "False" after each statement.

1. In the Olympics, Spitz had to beat some of the best swimmers in the world. ___True___

2. Spitz was just an average swimmer in the 1968 Olympics. _____

3. Nobody wanted Spitz to win in the '68 Olympic Games. _____

4. In 1972, Spitz wanted to win more gold medals. _____

5. In the 1972 Olympics, Spitz's performance was much better than the other swimmers'. _____

B. Get the Picture? Inferences

DIRECTIONS: An inference is something that is not stated directly, but is implied. Write "True" or "False" after each inference.

1. An athlete can be in the Olympic Games only one time. _____

2. The first-place medal is gold on the outside, but silver inside. _____

3. Companies pay Olympic winners a lot of money to advertise their products. _____

C. Get the Picture? Main Idea

DIRECTIONS: Mark the one statement that represents the main idea of the story.

1. ( ) Mark Spitz, the first athlete to win seven gold medals at the

same Olympic Games, made a lot of money because of his Olympic success.

2. (   ) Mark Spitz was wrong about the 1968 Olympic Games in Mexico City. He won two gold medals, but he said he would win six. So he tried again in 1972.

3. (   ) Mark Spitz was a good swimmer.

II.   MEANING EXERCISES

A.   Figure It Out

DIRECTIONS: Mark the meaning of the idiom underlined in each sentence.

1.   Jimmy Connors <u>was</u> so <u>good at</u> tennis that he played in all the big tournaments.

   a.   (   ) was nice during
   b.   (   ) tried hard at
   c.   (**x**) had much talent for

2.   Connors <u>competed against</u> some of the best players in the world, for example, Bjorn Borg, John McEnroe, and Ivan Lendl.

   a.   (   ) tried to beat in competition
   b.   (   ) didn't like during competition
   c.   (   ) was able to beat

3.   Connors was a fine tennis player and had a good sense of humor, so when he played a match, a lot of people would <u>root for</u> him.

   a.   (   ) watch constantly
   b.   (   ) express support for, cheer for
   c.   (   ) laugh at

4.   Every time Connors hit the ball, he seemed to <u>go for</u> a winning shot.

   a.   (   ) try not to get
   b.   (   ) try for
   c.   (   ) get

5. Jimmy Connors stands out as one of the great tennis players of all time.

   a. ( ) wants to be remembered
   b. ( ) is as tall
   c. ( ) is noticeable

B. What Does It Go With?

DIRECTIONS: Two of the three choices after each sentence can be correctly used with the idiom. Mark the *two* correct answers.

1. At the U.S. Open Tennis Tournament, fine tennis players compete against _____.

   a. (**x**) the best players from all over the world
   b. (**x**) each other
   c. ( ) tennis
   Hint: The object must be a person.

2. Linda is going to major in physics because she's good at _____.

   a. ( ) school
   b. ( ) science
   c. ( ) math
   Hint: The object must be a specific subject, sport, or skill.

3. Which _____ are you rooting for?

   a. ( ) sport
   b. ( ) soccer team
   c. ( ) runner
   Hint: The object must be a person or team.

4. Cynthia doesn't want to be an average runner; she always goes for _____.

   a. ( ) first place
   b. ( ) the finish line
   c. ( ) a gold medal
   Hint: The object must be something that represents success.

5. That _____ really stands out, so the
    judges gave her high scores.

     a. ( ) skater
     b. ( ) runner
     c. ( ) average gymnast

     Hint: The subject cannot be ordinary, because this contradicts the
     meaning of the idiom.

C. Look It Up

DIRECTIONS: Create your own minidictionary. For each idiom, write
the *meaning,* an appropriate *subject,* a *direct object* or *object of the
preposition* where indicated, and an *example sentence.* If you need
help, refer to the other exercises in this section. Notice the stress (/)
for each idiom, the position of the pronoun object [ ], and any special
grammar or stylistic notes.

When you have created your minidictionary for each chapter,
you can look an idiom up whenever you need to.

1. compéte agáinst [ ]
     Meaning: __try to beat in competition__
     Subject: __Bob's team__
     Object of preposition: __the state champions__
     Example sentence: __Bob's team is competing against__
     __the state champions.__

2. be góod at [ ]
     Meaning: _____
     Subject: _____
     Object of preposition: _____
     Example sentence: _____

3. róot for [ ]
     Meaning: _____
     Stylistic notes: __informal__
     Subject: _____
     Object of preposition: _____
     Example sentence: _____

4. go for [   ]

    Meaning: _____

    Grammar note: __object is often "it"_____

    Stylistic note: __informal_____

    Subject: _____

    Object of preposition: _____

    Example sentence: _____

5. stand out

    Meaning: _____

    Subject: _____

    Example sentence: _____

III.   GRAMMAR EXERCISES

A.   Fill It In: Prepositions and Particles

DIRECTIONS: Fill in the blanks with the correct prepositions or particles. Then play the tape and check your answers.

Tai Babylonia and Randy Gardner were good ____**at**____ fig-
                                                    1
ure skating. In fact, they stood _____ internationally in the
                                        2
world of ice skating.

In 1980, they decided to go _____ a Gold Medal in the
                                 3
Olympics. This wasn't going to be easy, because they would have to

compete _____ the Russians, Rodnina and Zaitzev. But Tai
             4
and Randy were so popular, everybody in the United States seemed to

be rooting _____ them.
                5
Just before the Olympic Games, Randy fell and the skaters couldn't
compete. What a disappointment!

B.   Fill It In: Object Pronouns

DIRECTIONS: In each sentence, fill in one of the blanks with the object pronoun in parentheses.

1.   The Romanian gymnasts are so good that the Americans are worried

about competing _____ against __**them**___. (them)
                              a   b

2.   Loraine has been playing the piano since she was a child. She's

very good _____ at _____. (it)
                        a   b

3.   Dave will be running in the New York City Marathon this year.

Are you going to go to the finish line to root _____ for
                                                               a

_____? (him)
      b

4.   If she wants to be an actress, she should go _____ for
                                                                  a

_____.   (it)
      b

IV.   LISTENING COMPREHENSION EXERCISE

A.   Listen In

DIRECTIONS: You will hear a situation presented in one or two sentences. Listen to each situation and mark the response here that most closely corresponds to the situation.

1.   a.   ( ) Terry always wants the American team to win.

     b.   (x) Terry never supports the American team.

     c.   ( ) Terry is patriotic.

2.   a.   ( ) Big Bob doesn't like competition.

     b.   ( ) Bob is only 10 years old.

     c.   ( ) Bob will beat the other boxer because Bob is much
              younger.

3. a. ( ) Elaine is not going to enter the competition next year because she doesn't think she can win.

    b. ( ) Elaine is sure she's going to win this year.

    c. ( ) Elaine will try to win next year.

4. a. ( ) Because Walter had been such a good manager, many employees expected him to become president.

    b. ( ) Walter was president of the company.

    c. ( ) Walter wasn't a very good manager.

5. a. ( ) Maria doesn't like politics.

    b. ( ) Maria has always had the talent for politics.

    c. ( ) When Maria was a child, her parents were politicians.

V. WRITING EXERCISE

A. Finish It Up

DIRECTIONS: Finish this entry in your diary. Use as many idioms as you can.

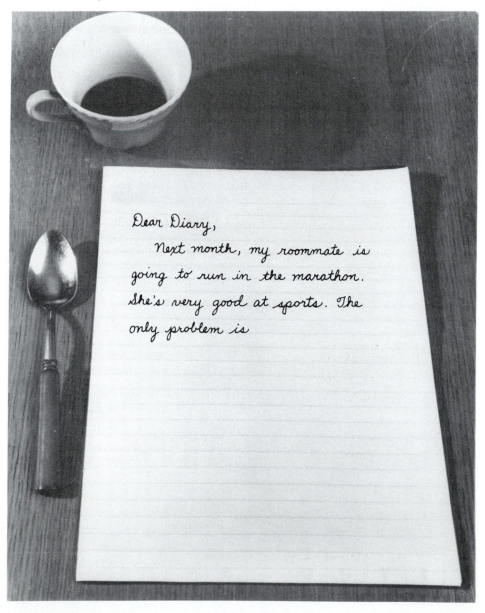

> Dear Diary,
>   Next month, my roommate is going to run in the marathon. She's very good at sports. The only problem is

VI. CONVERSATION ACTIVITIES

A. Act It Out

DIRECTIONS: Read each of the following situations and act it out. Use as many idioms as possible. Work with a partner.

be good at	root for
compete against	stand out
go for	

a. Your friend is a secretary in a busy advertising agency. Her boss, the office manager, is leaving the company. She wants the job but is afraid to say so. Give her advice and encouragement. For example, say, "Nancy, when Mr. Lipton leaves the company, you should go for his job."

b. You're the coach of a college basketball team. Your team has already lost five out of five games this season. Give the team advice before the next game.

c. Choose a sport you like. Pretend you're a television sportscaster and interview one particular player.

B. Talk It Over

Move around the room and find a class-mate who . . .

Write his or her name here.

a. always roots for athletes from his or her country. _____

b. is good at wind surfing. _____

c. hates to compete against anybody. _____

d. always goes for first place. _____

e. really stood out in school. _____

-2-

As you can see,
we all grew up
wearing sunglasses.

2 FAMILY

WARM-UP EXERCISE

- Find all the people in the class who have the same size family as you. For example, if there are three children in your family, find all those who have three children in their families.

- If you are the oldest child, find all those who are the oldest in their families. Use these categories:

  the oldest child
  the middle child
  one of the middle children
  the youngest child
  an only child

- Show the class a picture of yourself as a child. If possible, the picture should include other family members. Describe the picture.

READING SELECTION

DIRECTIONS: Read the following story silently. Then do the reading exercises that follow.

Growing Up

On June 21, 1983, everybody was crying in the delivery room[1] of the hospital, even the doctors. That day, Pam Peizer **gave birth to** six babies.

Unfortunately, one baby died, but four boys and one girl lived. Soon, everyone heard the news about the five babies, the Peizer quintuplets.

When the babies came home from the hospital, it wasn't easy to **tell** them **apart.** The Peizers would just count them to be sure all five babies were there.

At first, both Pam and Danny stayed home to **take care of** the quintuplets. Later, while the children were **growing up,** Danny stayed home with them while his wife went to work. The Peizers also had two baby nurses, and often the grandparents helped with the babysitting. But even with a lot of help, it's not easy to **bring up** five children, especially when they're all the same age.

It wasn't an accident that Pam Peizer had so many babies. She had quintuplets because she took a special drug called "pergeno." Although there are fertility drugs like the one Pam Peizer took, it's still unusual to have quintuplets. Fewer than fifty families in the world have quintuplets.

---

1. The room in a hospital where babies are born.

I.   READING EXERCISES

A.   Get the Picture? Comprehension

DIRECTIONS: These questions are based on the story you just read. Write "True" or "False" after each statement.

1.   Six babies were born to Pam Peizer on June 21, 1983.   __**True**__

2.   The quintuplets looked very similar.   _____

3.   In the beginning, Pam was the only babysitter.   _____

4.   Danny stayed home with the children only when they were very young.   _____

5.   Because Danny had a lot of help, it was easy to raise the children.   _____

B.   Get the Picture? Inferences

DIRECTIONS: An inference is something that is not stated directly, but is implied. Write "True" or "False" after each inference.

1.   Pam Peizer thought she was going to have more than one baby.   _____

2.   Pam and Danny Peizer are a traditional couple.   _____

3.   The children's grandparents live near the Peizers.   _____

C.   Get the Picture? Main Idea

DIRECTIONS: Mark the one statement that represents the main idea of the story.

1.   (   ) Danny Peizer is a good father.

2.   (   ) Parents of large families should have babysitters to help them with their children.

3. ( ) Something unusual happened on June 21, 1983: Pam Peizer had quintuplets.

II. MEANING EXERCISES

A. Figure It Out

DIRECTIONS: Mark the meaning of the idiom underlined in each sentence.

1. Laurette just <u>gave birth to</u> fraternal twins.

    a. ( ) helped deliver
    b. (**x**) produced, was delivered of
    c. ( ) was born as one of two

2. Because the babies are fraternal twins, they look different. If they were identical twins, it wouldn't be so easy to <u>tell</u> them <u>apart</u>.

    a. ( ) be able to see the difference between them
    b. ( ) keep them in separate places
    c. ( ) talk to them separately

3. The twins are so cute that everyone wants to <u>take care of</u> them.

    a. ( ) look at
    b. ( ) take home, keep permanently
    c. ( ) take responsibility for, watch

4. Instead of getting a baby nurse, Laurette wants to <u>bring up</u> the children herself.

    a. ( ) raise, educate
    b. ( ) feed, nourish
    c. ( ) carry

5. Laurette wants to see them <u>grow up</u>.

    a. ( ) crawl around
    b. ( ) eat their food
    c. ( ) become older and bigger

B. What Does It Go With?

DIRECTIONS: Two of the three choices after each sentence can be correctly used with the idiom. Mark the *two* correct answers.

1. Fred's wife just gave birth to _____ .

   a. (   ) a baby
   b. (**x**) a baby girl
   c. (**x**) twins
   Hint: The answer should not be part of the meaning of the idiom. New information should be given.

2. Tony and his brother Jim look so much alike that it's impossible to tell _____ apart.

   a. (   ) the two brothers
   b. (   ) the older one
   c. (   ) the boys
   Hint: The object must be two or more people.

3. It isn't easy for a single parent to work full time and take care of _____ too.

   a. (   ) television
   b. (   ) three children
   c. (   ) a house
   Hint: The object must be a person or thing that needs attention.

4. Where did _____ grow up?

   a. (   ) your cat
   b. (   ) your children
   c. (   ) your girlfriend
   Hint: The subject must be a person or people.

5. _____ was brought up by her grandparents.

   a. (   ) Her older sister
   b. (   ) Her daughter
   c. (   ) Her doll
   Hint: The subject[2] must be a person.

2. This is the subject of a passive sentence. In an active sentence, it would be the object.

C.   Look It Up

DIRECTIONS: Create your own minidictionary. For each idiom, write the *meaning*, an appropriate *subject*, a *direct object* or *object of the preposition* where indicated, and an *example sentence*. If you need help, refer to the other exercises in this section. Notice the stress (/) for each idiom, the position of the pronoun object [ ], and any special grammar or stylistic notes.

When you have created your minidictionary for each chapter, you can look an idiom up whenever you need to.

1. give birth, give birth to [ ]

Meaning: __produce, be delivered of, bear__

Subject: __Tom's wife__

Object of preposition: __a baby boy__

Example sentence: __Tom's wife just gave birth to a beautiful baby boy.__

2. tell [ ] apart

Meaning: _____

Grammar notes: __often with "can" or "can't"__

Subject: _____

Direct object: _____

Example sentence: _____

3. take care, take care of [ ]

Meaning: _____

Subject: _____

Object of preposition: _____

Example sentence: _____

4. grow up

Meaning: _____

Subject: _____

Example sentence: _____

5. bring [ ] up

      Meaning: _____

      Grammar note: _often passive_____

      Subject: _____

      Direct object: _____

      Example sentence: _____

III. GRAMMAR EXERCISES

A. Fill It In: Prepositions and Particles

> DIRECTIONS: Fill in the blanks with the correct prepositions or particles. Then play the tape and check your answers.

On January 12, 1988, Michele L'Esperance gave birth __to__
                                              1

quintuplets. Four were girls—Veronica, Erica, Alexandria, and
Danielle—and one was a boy, Raymond. It wasn't easy to tell them

_____.
   2

After the quintuplets were born, the doctors and nurses in the
hospital had to take care _____ them for two months. These
                                  3
weren't ordinary quintuplets; they were the first test-tube quintuplets
born in the United States.

The quintuplets will be brought _____ in Clarkstown,
                                           4
Michigan. Everyone hopes they will grow _____ and be
                                           5
healthy children.

B. Fill It In: Object Pronouns

DIRECTIONS: In each sentence, fill in *one* of the blanks with the object pronoun in parentheses.

1. Dorothy's husband was very excited about the twins when she

    gave _____ birth to __**them**__. (them)
         a   b

2. Those two sisters look so much alike that it isn't easy to tell

    _____ apart _____. (them)
         a   b

3. Joan is 80 years old, but she doesn't want anyone to take

    _____ care of _____. (her)
         a   b

4. When Tom's wife died, his children were worried that he would

    get married again. He didn't; he brought _____ up
                                                    a

    _____ (them) by himself.
         b

IV. LISTENING COMPREHENSION EXERCISE

A. Listen In

DIRECTIONS: You will hear a situation presented in one or two sentences. Listen to each situation and mark the response here that most closely corresponds to the situation.

1. a. ( ) Paul wants to get a babysitter.

    b. ( ) Barbara wants to be a babysitter.

    c. (**x**) Paul wants Barbara to stay with their daughter during the day.

2. a. ( ) Frank lived in London when he was young.

b. ( ) Frank was born in London.

c. ( ) Frank's parents took him to London for a visit when he was young.

3. a. ( ) Diane and her sister are twins.

   b. ( ) Diane is going to have a baby boy.

   c. ( ) Diane is going to produce twins.

4. a. ( ) Michael and James look the same except for Michael's birthmark.

   b. ( ) Michael and James are always together.

   c. ( ) James and Michael both have birthmarks.

5. a. ( ) Nancy joined the army when she got older.

   b. ( ) Nancy lived in Texas when she was young.

   c. ( ) Nancy has always lived in Massachusetts.

V. WRITING EXERCISE

A. Finish It Up

DIRECTIONS: Finish this entry in your diary. Use the following information and as many idioms as you can.

- The Kienast quintuplets were born on February 28, 1969.
- They lived in New Jersey.
- In 1983, their father committed suicide.
- The quintuplets have been in TV commercials.

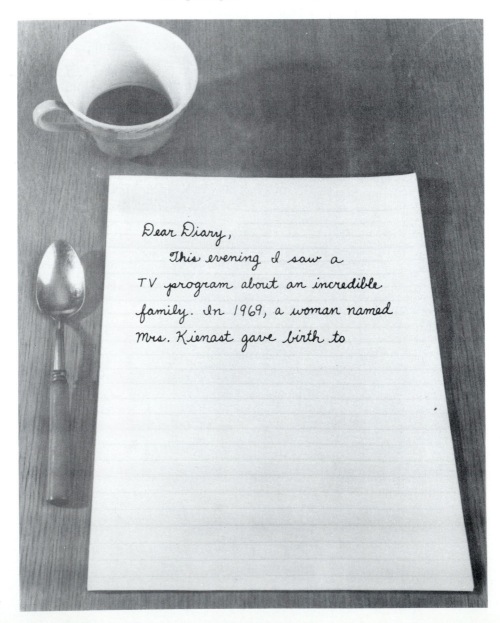

Dear Diary,
    This evening I saw a
TV program about an incredible
family. In 1969, a woman named
Mrs. Kienast gave birth to

VI. CONVERSATION ACTIVITIES

A. Act It Out

DIRECTIONS: Read each of the following situations and act it out. Use as many idioms as possible. Work with a partner.

bring up	take care of
give birth to	tell apart
grow up	

1. Your wife (or you) just had twins. Call your parents to tell them the good news. For example, say, "Mom, guess what! Ginny just gave birth to twins!"

2. You can't have children, and you want to adopt a baby. You go to an adoption agency and talk with a social worker. The social worker asks you why you want to adopt a baby and how you plan to raise the child.

3. You and your husband (or wife) fight every day. Both of you finally decide to go for counseling. The marriage counselor asks you to talk about your childhood.

B. Talk It Over

1. Move around the room and find a classmate who . . .

   Write his or her name here.

   a. had to take care of younger brothers or sisters when he or she was a child.
   _____

   b. was brought up by a single parent.
   _____

   c. grew up in a small town.
   _____

   d. knows someone who has given birth to more than five children.
   _____

e. can't tell two other students apart.   _____

Which students?   _____ and _____

2. Discuss the following topics in a small group. Write your answers, and then share them with the class.

a. What are the advantages or disadvantages of being a twin?

An advantage: _____

A disadvantage: _____

b. Who should bring up the children: the mother, the father, both parents, the grandparents, a paid babysitter?

_____

Give three reasons for your answer:

1. _____

2. _____

3. _____

c. Is it better to be the only child in the family or to have brothers

and sisters?   _____

Why?   _____

_____

d. What was the hardest thing for you about growing up?

_____

_____

e. When you were growing up, what was fun for you? Write three things:

1. _____

2. _____

3. _____

3 COMMUNICATION

WARM-UP EXERCISE

Write your first name on a small piece of paper. (Write the name you want your classmates to call you during the course.) Next, write two adjectives that describe you. For example:

BOB	friendly	funny

Tape your paper to your clothes. Walk around the room and read your classmates' names and adjectives. Ask two students for their telephone numbers and write their names and numbers below.

_____   _____
Name   Telephone

_____   _____
Name   Telephone

READING SELECTION

DIRECTIONS: Read the following story silently. Then do the reading exercises that follow.

Get in Touch

Jim Peterson was planning a trip to Italy. The problem was that he didn't know Italian. Two months before his trip, he **called up** Phone Lab, a language school,[1] and said he wanted to study Italian. This is what the school told him about its language courses:

Every day at a certain time, your Italian teacher will **get in touch with** you by phone, at work or at home. If you**'re on the phone** at that time, you have to **hang up** so your teacher can **get through.** Each class is thirty minutes long. Don't worry, Phone Lab pays the telephone bill.

Once a month, there's a party with your teacher and the other students studying Italian. After you've met the other students, you can **keep in touch with** them by phone, too.

Jim liked this idea and took an eight-week telephone course. When he arrived in Italy, he had no problem with the language. Jim had married his Italian teacher the day before the trip, so she was on the trip with him.

Phone Lab doesn't promise everyone the same success as Jim, but it does promise a good language course by phone.

---

1. There really is a language school called "Phone Lab" in New York City.

I. READING EXERCISES

A. Get the Picture? Comprehension

DIRECTIONS: These questions are based on the story you just read. Write "True" or "False" after each statement.

1. Jim contacted Phone Lab for information about its language courses.   _____True_____

2. The students call the teacher for class.   _____

3. If your phone is busy when it's time for your class, you should end the conversation so your teacher can reach you.   _____

4. After meeting at the parties, students can't call each other.   _____

B. Get the Picture? Inferences

DIRECTIONS: An inference is something that is not stated directly, but is implied. Write "True" or "False" after each inference.

1. Only the student speaks Italian over the phone.   _____

2. Jim's new wife helped him with the language in Italy.   _____

3. Phone Lab teaches different languages by phone.   _____

C. Get the Picture? Main Idea

DIRECTIONS: Mark the one statement that represents the main idea of the story.

1. (   ) Jim Peterson needed to learn Italian before his trip to Italy.

2. (   ) Phone Lab offers language courses by telephone.

3. (   ) Phone Lab teaches Italian.

II. MEANING EXERCISES

A. Figure It Out

DIRECTIONS: Mark the meaning of the idiom underlined in each sentence.

1. Every time Bill <u>calls up</u> Martha, he has a problem.

    a. (   ) talks to in person
    b. (**x**) contacts by telephone
    c. (   ) screams at

2. Martha has so many secretaries in her laboratory that Bill can never <u>get in touch with</u> her.

    a. (   ) hear
    b. (   ) contact, communicate with
    c. (   ) understand completely

3. The secretaries always say Martha <u>is on the phone</u> or in a meeting.

    a. (   ) is talking on the phone
    b. (   ) has a telephone
    c. (   ) doesn't want to talk on the phone

4. After Bill talks to the third secretary, he usually gets angry and <u>hangs up</u>.

    a. (   ) puts down the telephone receiver
    b. (   ) screams
    c. (   ) tries to kill himself

5. Martha told Bill to say that he's Doctor William Harris when he calls, and he'll have no problem <u>getting through</u>.

    a. (   ) getting his test results
    b. (   ) getting a secretary
    c. (   ) reaching her by phone

6. After Bill started calling himself "doctor," it was easy for him to get in touch with Martha and to <u>keep in touch with</u> her.

    a. (   ) continue talking to
    b. (   ) see
    c. (   ) have regular contact with

B.   What Does It Go With?

DIRECTIONS: Two of the three choices after each sentence can be correctly used with the idiom. Mark the *two* correct answers.

1.   Angela calls _____ up every day.

       a.   (**x**) her mother
       b.   (   ) her dog
       c.   (**x**) her best friend
      Hint: The object must be a person or persons.

2.   When you arrive in Dallas, get in touch with _____.

       a.   (   ) your office assistant
       b.   (   ) Helen
       c.   (   ) the telephone book
      Hint: The object must be a person.

3.   _____ is on the phone every time I try to call her.

       a.   (   ) My sister
       b.   (   ) Her number
       c.   (   ) Her teenage son
      Hint: The subject must be a person.

4.   In the middle of the conversation, _____ suddenly hung up.

       a.   (   ) the telephone
       b.   (   ) her boyfriend
       c.   (   ) her secretary
      Hint: The subject must be a person.

5.   _____ couldn't get through last night.

       a.   (   ) The overseas operator
       b.   (   ) Joe's wife
       c.   (   ) The telephone
      Hint: The subject must be a person.

6.   Don't forget to keep in touch with _____.

    a.   ( ) the people you work with every day
    b.   ( ) your old friends
    c.   ( ) each other

Hint: The object must be people you don't see regularly.

C.   Look It Up

DIRECTIONS: Create your own minidictionary. For each idiom, write the *meaning*, an appropriate *subject*, a *direct object* or *object of the preposition* where indicated, and an *example sentence*. If you need help, refer to the other exercises in this section. Notice the stress (/) for each idiom, the position of the pronoun object [   ], and any special grammar or stylistic notes.

When you have created your minidictionary for each chapter, you can look an idiom up whenever you need to.

1.   call [   ] up

    Meaning: __telephone__

    Subject: __I, Judy, her brother__

    Direct object: __my sister__

    Example sentence: __I called my sister up as soon as I heard the good news.__

2.   get in touch, get in touch with [   ]

    Meaning: _____

    Subject: _____

    Object of preposition: _____

    Example sentence: _____

3.   be on the phone

    Meaning: _____

    Subject: _____

    Example sentence: _____

4. hang up, hang [　] up

    Meaning: _____

    Subject: _____

    Direct object: ___the phone, the receiver____

    Example sentence: _____

5. get through, get through to [　]

    Meaning: _____

    Subject: _____

    Object of preposition: _____

    Example sentence: _____

6. keep in touch, keep in touch with [　]

    Meaning: _____

    Grammar note: ___often imperative: Keep in touch!___

    Subject: _____

    Object of preposition: _____

    Example sentence: _____

III. GRAMMAR EXERCISES

A. Fill It In: Prepositions and Particles

DIRECTIONS: Fill in the blanks with the correct prepositions or particles. Then play the tape and check your answers.

Do you think it's difficult to meet new people? If you do, you may be ready to place a personal ad in a local magazine or newspaper. After you place your ad, anyone can get ____in____ touch

_____ you by writing to the magazine. The magazine then
    2

sends you all the letters, and you can call _____ the people
                                3

you want to meet. If you don't like how they sound, you can say "good-

bye" and hang _____ quickly. If you like how they sound,
              4

you arrange a date. And, if you like the first date, you can keep

_____ touch _____ each other and continue dating.
    5   6

B. Fill It In: Object Pronouns

DIRECTIONS: In each sentence, fill in *one* of the blanks with the object pronoun in parentheses.

1. If you like her, you should call _____**her**_____ up

   _____. (her)
      b

2. During Dorothy's vacation, her secretary couldn't get in touch

   _____ with _____. (her)
      a   b

3. Would you please take the receiver and hang _____ up
                                                     a

   _____. (it)
      b

4. When you return to Los Angeles, try to keep in touch

   _____ with _____. (us)
      a   b

IV. LISTENING COMPREHENSION EXERCISE

A. Listen In

DIRECTIONS: You will hear a situation presented in one or two sentences. Listen to each situation and mark the response here that most closely corresponds to the situation.

1. a. ( ) The police answered the phone immediately, but it was too late for the woman.

   b. (**x**) The police probably had many other emergency calls at the same time.

   c. ( ) The police couldn't contact Joe.

2. a. ( ) It's necessary to call your friends regularly.

   b. ( ) Good friends understand if you're too busy to call them.

   c. ( ) Good friends like it when you touch them.

3. a. ( ) It was easier for Bruno to talk over the phone than in person.

   b. ( ) It was easier for Bruno to talk in person than over the phone.

   c. ( ) Bruno didn't know anyone to call when he came from Italy.

4. a. ( ) A lot of people have answering machines.

   b. ( ) A lot of people leave a message on her answering machine.

   c. ( ) A lot of people don't leave a message on her answering machine.

5. a. ( ) Janet is a writer.

   b. ( ) Janet would like to call or send a letter to her favorite writer.

   c. ( ) Janet doesn't know how to write.

6. a. ( ) Doris's phone was broken.

   b. ( ) Doris was talking to Doug on the phone all night.

   c. ( ) Doris was talking to somebody else for a long time.

V. WRITING EXERCISE

A. Finish It Up

DIRECTIONS: Finish this entry in your diary. Use as many idioms as you can.

VI.   CONVERSATION ACTIVITIES

A.   Act It Out

> DIRECTIONS: Read each of the following situations and act it out. Use as many idioms as possible. Work with a partner.

be on the phone	get in touch with	hang up
call up	get through	keep in touch with

1. You're having a big party. Several guests are coming to the party by train. You want them to call you from the station so you can drive them to the party. Tell one guest what he or she should do after getting off the train. For example, say, "When you get off the train, go to the store and call me up. If . . ."

2. Your best friend recently met a woman that he wants to date. He took her phone number and tried to call her a few times, but the phone was always busy. Now he's a little shy about calling her, but he still wants to ask her for a date. Discuss it with him.

3. Your wife (or husband) calls you at your office and says she (or he) has just seen somebody get shot on the street. She doesn't know what to do. You think she should call the police. Discuss it with her.

4. You work for your government's Secret Service. You're sending a member of your team to another country to do a special job. You know it's a dangerous job, and you want the agent to contact you regularly. You don't want anyone to hear the agent talking to you, however. Give your agent advice on how to call you.

B.   Talk It Over

> DIRECTIONS: Discuss the following topics in a small group. Write your answers. Then share them with the class.

1. Give at least three reasons why it seems more difficult to speak and understand a foreign language over the phone than in person.

   1. _____**It's harder to hear the other person's voice.**_____

2. _____

3. _____

2. Who do you call in case of the following emergencies?

   a fire _____ , a car accident _____ ,

   a robbery _____ , a serious sickness _____ .

   What do you do if you can't get through? _____

   _____

3. Some people call up their friends regularly, even if they live far away. Other people rarely call up their friends. It doesn't mean that they don't like them; it's just that they have trouble keeping in touch.

   Which type are you? _____

   _____

   What do you think about your type? _____

   _____

   What do you think about the other type? _____

   _____

4. Not only language classes are available by phone. Psychotherapy and counseling are available by phone, too. An advertisement for such therapy is on the following page.

   What do you think of psychotherapy by phone? _____

   _____

   _____

Dr. Lydia Gardner, Psychotherapist
PERSONAL AND MARRIAGE COUNSELOR
1008 Third Avenue
NEW YORK, N.Y.
PSYCHOTHERAPY AND COUNSELING BY PHONE
(212) 245-8625   IF BUSY: (212) 822-3640

LOVE, RELATIONSHIP, AND
MARRIAGE THERAPY

SEPARATION AND DIVORCE

SINGLES' LIFESTYLE
PROBLEMS

STRESS, ANXIETY, AND
DEPRESSION

FEELINGS OF ISOLATION AND
LONELINESS

SPECIAL PROBLEMS OF
CAREER WOMEN
AND MEN

SPECIAL PROBLEMS OF
ARTISTS AND
PERFORMERS

If you need instant advice or help, just call us up and you'll
be able to get through to a therapist immediately or within
minutes. And you can be on the phone as long as you want. No
appointment is necessary for consultation by phone, and you can
call from home, office, or anywhere Mon. – Sat. from 7 A.M. to 9 P.M.

Your consultation will be charged to your credit card at the rate
of 15 minutes: $25; 30 minutes: $50; 45 minutes: $75, etc. Please
have your credit card ready when you call.

What other services are available by phone?   _____

_____

_____

4 EDUCATION

Everyone learns to speak his or her own language, but not everyone learns to read that language. What three things could you do to help people learn to read?

1. _____

2. _____

3. _____

READING SELECTION

DIRECTIONS: Read the following story silently. Then do the reading exercises that follow.

Dropping Out

A personal problem has become a national problem, and it's getting bigger and bigger. It's not drugs, and it's not drunk drivers. The problem is illiteracy.[1]

About 26 million Americans are functionally illiterate. In other words, they can't **fill out** job applications because they can't read the forms, and they can't **figure out** the directions on food packages or understand simple newspaper articles.

Many illiterates[2] aren't **working on** their problem because they're too embarrassed about it. They don't want their friends or their children to know that they can't read.

But some people are doing something about this national problem. The Coalition for Literacy, a group of eleven literacy organizations that includes Literacy Volunteers[3] of America, Inc., and Laubach Literacy Action, has **focused on** the problem and gives help with reading across the country.

Illiterates are **signing up for** free tutoring[4] in almost every state, but some people think the illiteracy problem will never end. While volunteers are teaching adults to read, children with reading problems are **dropping out of** school because they can't **keep up with** their classmates. And, although it is hard to believe, some high schools give diplomas to functional illiterates. Unfortunately, the children with reading problems today will be illiterate adults tomorrow.

1. The inability to read or write.
2. People unable to read or write.
3. Volunteers are people who give their free time to help others.
4. A class situation in which one teacher works with one student.

I. READING EXERCISES

A. Get the Picture? Comprehension

DIRECTIONS: These questions are based on the story you just read. Write "True" or "False" after each statement.

1. It's easy for illiterates to answer the questions on job applications.   **False**

2. Functional illiterates can understand the directions on food packages.   _____

3. Many illiterates aren't doing anything about their problem because they're embarrassed about it.   _____

4. The Coalition for Literacy is trying to do something about the illiteracy problem.   _____

5. Illiterates are not registering for tutoring.   _____

6. Many children stop going to school because they have reading problems.   _____

7. Children with reading problems are as successful as other children in school.   _____

B. Get the Picture? Inferences

DIRECTIONS: An inference is something that is not stated directly, but is implied. Write "True" or "False" after each inference.

1. All high schools in the United States do a good job of teaching students.   _____

2. Being illiterate makes it difficult to get a job.   _____

3. Some literacy groups give free tutoring for adults.   _____

C. Get the Picture? Main Idea

DIRECTIONS: Mark the one statement that represents the main idea of the story.

1. ( ) The 26 million Americans who are functionally illiterate have trouble reading application forms, newspaper articles, and directions on food packages.

2. ( ) Although literacy volunteers in every state are teaching adults to read, illiteracy continues to be a big problem in the United States.

3. ( ) It's embarrassing to be illiterate.

II. MEANING EXERCISES

A. Figure It Out

DIRECTIONS: Mark the meaning of the idiom underlined in each sentence.

1. When Judy applied for a passport, she had to <u>fill out</u> a lot of forms.

  a. ( ) ask for in writing
  b. ( ) present
  c. (**x**) complete in writing

2. When Judy gave the forms to the clerk, he said he couldn't <u>figure out</u> her answers.

  a. ( ) understand
  b. ( ) translate
  c. ( ) find

3. The clerk said she should <u>work on</u> her penmanship.

  a. ( ) make money through
  b. ( ) give thought and effort to
  c. ( ) buy a new pen to improve

4. Judy said he should <u>focus on</u> her application, so she could get home to her computer.

    a. ( ) take a picture of
    b. ( ) look at
    c. ( ) concentrate on

5. When the clerk asked why Judy wanted to get home to her computer, she said she had just <u>signed up for</u> a computer course and wanted to practice on her new computer.

    a. ( ) asked for information about, inquired about
    b. ( ) registered for, joined
    c. ( ) stopped attending

6. The clerk said he signed up for a computer course once but <u>dropped out</u> because he already knew everything.

    a. ( ) dropped the computer on the floor
    b. ( ) stopped participating before the end
    c. ( ) went outside

7. Under her breath, Judy said he probably dropped out because he couldn't <u>keep up with</u> the other students in the class.

    a. ( ) understand any of
    b. ( ) communicate with
    c. ( ) stay at the same level as

B. What Does It Go With?

DIRECTIONS: Two of the three choices after each sentence can be correctly used with the idiom. Mark the **two** correct answers.

1. If you want to apply for the job, you have to fill out

_____.

    a. (**x**) this form
    b. ( ) the office
    c. (**x**) an application
    Hint: The object must be a written form to be completed.

2. I can't figure out _____.

    a. ( ) a solution to the problem
    b. ( ) teenagers
    c. ( ) the number "five"
    Hint: The object must be someone or something difficult to understand.

3. Margaret's husband has finally decided to work on

    _____.

    a. ( ) the morning
    b. ( ) his weight problem
    c. ( ) his book
    Hint: The object must be a specific problem or project.

4. Gerry is trying to focus on _____.

    a. ( ) his vacation plans
    b. ( ) his project for school
    c. ( ) everything he's doing in his life
    Hint: The object must be a specific problem or project.

5. If you want to learn how to play the piano, why don't you sign

    up for _____?

    a. ( ) the music office
    b. ( ) piano lessons
    c. ( ) a course
    Hint: The object must be a course or class.

6. George has trouble finishing things. He dropped out of

    _____ a month before graduation.

    a. ( ) college
    b. ( ) school
    c. ( ) his homework
    Hint: The object must be a course or academic institution.

7. Jane started exercise classes, but couldn't keep up with

    _____.

    a. ( ) herself
    b. ( ) the rest of the class
    c. ( ) the teacher
    Hint: The object must be someone different from the subject.

C.   Look It Up

DIRECTIONS: Create your own minidictionary. For each idiom, **write** the *meaning*, an appropriate *subject*, a *direct object* or *object of the preposition* where indicated, and an *example sentence*. If you **need** help, refer to the other exercises in this section. Notice the **stress** (/) for each idiom, the position of the pronoun object [ ], and any **special** grammar or stylistic notes.

When you have created your minidictionary for **each chapter,** you can look an idiom up whenever you need to.

1. fill [ ] out
    Meaning: __complete (a form) in writing__
    Subject: __you, the patient__
    Direct object: __a form, an application form__
    Example sentence: __To get a license, you have to fill out a__
    __form.__

2. figure [ ] out
    Meaning: _____
    Grammar note: __often negative (with "can't")__
    Stylistic note: __informal__
    Subject: _____
    Direct object: _____
    Example sentence: _____

3. work on [   ]

    Meaning: _____

    Subject: _____

    Object of preposition: _____

    Example sentence: _____

4. focus on [   ], focus [   ] on [   ]

    Meaning: _____

    Subject: _____

    Direct object: _____

    Object of preposition: _____

    Example sentence: _____

5. sign up, sign up for [   ]

    Meaning: _____

    Subject: _____

    Object of preposition: _____

    Example sentence: _____

6. drop out, drop out of [   ]

    Meaning: _____

    Stylistic note: __informal_____

    Subject: _____

    Object of preposition: _____

    Example sentence: _____

7. keep up, keep up with [   ]

    Meaning: _____

    Subject: _____

    Object of preposition: _____

    Example sentence: _____

III. GRAMMAR EXERCISES

A. Fill It In: Prepositions and Particles

> DIRECTIONS: Fill in the blanks with the correct prepositions or particles. Then play the tape and check your answers.

Ellen wanted to be a Spanish-English translator, so she signed

_____**up**_____   _____   a course in translation. To take the
    1   2

course, she had to fill   _____   an application form and answer
                          3

questions in the two languages.

In the first class, the students had to work   _____   trans-
                         4

lating a newspaper article from Spanish to English. It wasn't easy. In

fact, Ellen couldn't even figure   _____   the title of the article!
                         5

For homework, the class had to translate a poem by Pablo Neruda

into English. Poor Ellen! She tried to focus   _____   the mean-
                         6

ing of the whole poem, but she had a lot of trouble.

By the second day, Ellen was ready to drop   _____
                         7

_____   the course. The other students didn't have any trouble
    8

with the homework, and Ellen knew it was going to be difficult to keep

_____   _____   the group.
    9   10

Today, Ellen is a professional cook. The only thing she has to

translate is recipes!

B. `Fill It In: Object Pronouns

DIRECTIONS: In each sentence, fill in *one* of the blanks with the object pronoun in parentheses.

1. You don't have much time to send in your application. As soon as you get the form, fill _____**it**_____ out _____. (it)
    _a   _b

2. If you don't know the meaning of a word, look at the sentence it's in and try to figure _____ out _____. (it)
    _a   _b

3. When Ann didn't get her paycheck, she called the Payroll Office. The manager said someone was working _____ on
    _a

    _____. (it)
    _b

4. Unemployment is a big problem. I don't understand why the government doesn't focus _____ on _____. (it)
    _a   _b

5. You'll never take that computer science course if you don't sign up _____ for _____ (it) today.
    _a   _b

6. Terry's job involves so much paperwork that she's having trouble keeping _____ up with _____. (it)
    _a   _b

IV. LISTENING COMPREHENSION EXERCISE

A. Listen In

DIRECTIONS: You will hear a situation presented in one or two sentences. Listen to each situation and mark the response here that most closely corresponds to the situation.

1. a. ( ) Kevin completed the application form but didn't get the job.

b. (**x**) Kevin didn't complete the form.

c. ( ) Kevin completed the application form and got the job.

2. a. ( ) Elizabeth was the quickest one to understand the problem.

b. ( ) Elizabeth couldn't understand the first problem.

c. ( ) Elizabeth has a good figure.

3. a. ( ) Timothy is ready to play in the concert.

b. ( ) Timothy needs more practice.

c. ( ) Timothy doesn't want to work; he wants to play.

4. a. ( ) Donna is concentrating on her work and her children.

b. ( ) Donna can't concentrate on her work or her children because her husband is sick.

c. ( ) Donna is upset about her work and her children.

5. a. ( ) All senior citizens get meals delivered to their homes, even if they don't ask for them.

b. ( ) Meals on Wheels is a place where senior citizens can go to get their meals.

c. ( ) Senior citizens can get their meals delivered if they register for the service.

6. a. ( ) Carl left school in his second year, but returned years later to finish his Bachelor's degree and then get a Master's degree.

b. ( ) Carl completed college in two years.

c. ( ) Carl never finished college.

7. a. ( ) Robert makes everybody walk as fast as he does.

b. ( ) Robert can't continue walking so fast.

c. ( ) Nobody can walk at the same speed as Robert.

V. WRITING EXERCISE

A. Finish It Up

DIRECTIONS: Finish this entry in your diary. Use as many idioms as you can.

Dear Diary,
     I'm bored. I think I'll sign up for

VI. CONVERSATION ACTIVITIES

A. Act It Out

DIRECTIONS: Read each of the following situations and act it out. Use as many idioms as possible. Work with a partner.

drop out	fill out	sign up for
figure out	focus on	work on
	keep up with	

1. You want to register for an English course, so you go to a language school and talk to the secretary. Tell her that you want to improve your accent — that is, that you want a course in pronunciation. Also, ask if you can get your money back if you don't like the course or if the other students are more advanced than you. For example, say, "Hello, I'd like to sign up for an English course . . ."

2. You've been working too hard and not getting any exercise. You decide to become a member of a health club and to take an exercise class. Ask the manager of the club for information.

3. You've never been able to dance, and finally you're going to do something about it. You saw an ad in the newspaper for small-group lessons. Call and get the information you need.

B. Talk It Over

1. Move around the room and find a classmate who . . .

   Write his or her name here.

   a. wants to work on conversation skills in English.

   _____

   b. has signed up for — and fin-ished — at least three English courses in the past.

   _____

   c. has dropped out of at least one English course in the past.

   _____

d. had trouble filling out the application form for this English course.   _____

e. still can't figure out when to use "make" and "do" in English.   _____

f. thinks an English course should focus on vocabulary.   _____

g. is having trouble keeping up with the other students in this class.   _____

2. Discuss the following topics in a small group. Write your answers and then share them with the class.

a. Which other countries, besides the United States, have literacy problems?

_____

_____

_____

_____

b. What else can be done about illiteracy besides tutoring?

_____

_____

_____

c. Do you read a lot?   ( ) yes   ( ) no

What do you read?   ( ) books   ( ) science fiction
                     ( ) magazines   ( ) biographies
                     ( ) newspapers   ( ) mysteries
                     ( ) _____   ( ) novels
                                           ( ) history

In general, do people in your country read a lot?
( ) yes   ( ) no

How do you know?   _____

_____

5 FOOD

WARM-UP EXERCISE

Write three foods you love to eat:

first choice: _____

second choice: _____

third choice: _____

Are they good for you?

first choice: ( ) yes   ( ) no
second choice: ( ) yes   ( ) no
third choice: ( ) yes   ( ) no

Did you ever have a weight problem?   ( ) yes   ( ) no

Were you too fat or too thin?   _____

What did you do about it?   _____

_____

Share your answers with your group or the class.

READING SELECTION

DIRECTIONS: Read the following story silently. Then do the reading exercises that follow.

Polish It Off

Are you the type of person who **gulps down** every meal[1] in two minutes? Do you eat candy to **tide** you **over** between lunch and dinner? Do you **polish off** a big bag of potato chips by yourself? Would you like to **do without** sugar in your coffee, but can't? If you do any or all of these things, you need help from one of the many available diet products: diet pills, diet powders, diet foods, or diet books.

If you think Americans **are obsessed with** dieting, you're probably right. About 70 million Americans are overweight,[2] and more than half of them are trying to lose.

Many overweight people take diet pills. Taking diet pills controls your appetite, so you eat less. But are diet pills safe? Some researchers[3] say "no."

Another way you can lose weight is to take diet powders.[4] Diet powders can be **mixed with** water or skim milk.[5] They're good for you because they have vitamins[6] and minerals[7] and other substances the body needs. They help you lose weight because they have a limited number of calories. You can drink the powder mixture instead of eating a meal. This is an easy way to have a healthy meal while limiting the number of calories you **take in.**

But some people aren't satisfied unless they eat a real meal. Such people can buy low-salt, low-fat, frozen foods that look and taste like regular meals, but have a limited number of calories.

And then there are the diet books that tell you what to eat and what not to eat and list how many calories each food has. With the diet pills, the diet powders, the diet foods, and the diet books, dieting is becoming very complicated. But everybody knows how to lose weight: just eat less, exercise more, and **stick to** it!

1. Breakfast, lunch, or dinner.
2. Too heavy.
3. People who study a particular subject.
4. Dry, dustlike particles.
5. Milk with the cream removed.

6. Substances, found in foods, that are necessary for the body.
7. Substances, found in the earth, that are necessary for the body.

I. READING EXERCISES

A. Get the Picture? Comprehension

DIRECTIONS: These questions are based on the story you just read. Write "True" or "False" after each statement.

1. Some overweight people eat too fast. _____**True**_____

2. Overweight people often eat candy when they get hungry between meals. _____

3. People with weight problems never eat big bags of potato chips by themselves. _____

4. Some people must have sugar in their coffee. _____

5. Americans don't talk enough about dieting. _____

6. A diet powder is a powder that you eat with a spoon. _____

7. A diet powder limits the number of calories you consume. _____

8. To lose weight, it's necessary to continue to eat less and exercise more. _____

B. Get the Picture? Inferences

DIRECTIONS: An inference is something that is not stated directly, but is implied. Write "True" or "False" after each inference.

1. Diet pills are one of the most dangerous ways to lose weight. _____

2. Many overweight Americans can't just eat less and exercise more to lose weight. They need help. _____

3. Diet products are not a big business in the United States. _____

C. Get the Picture? Main Idea

DIRECTIONS: Mark the one statement that represents the main idea of the story.

1. ( ) Many Americans need to go on a diet.

2. ( ) There are many products available to help people who want to lose weight. To lose, people must eat right and exercise regularly.

3. ( ) Diet pills can be dangerous, and some people don't like diet powders. To lose weight, diet foods are the best for most people.

II. MEANING EXERCISES

A. Figure It Out

DIRECTIONS: Mark the meaning of the idiom underlined in each sentence.

1. George is one of the 70 million Americans who are overweight. He does everything wrong. He gulps down two cheeseburgers at his desk every day at 12:00 P.M.

    a. (**x**) swallows (food or drink) quickly
    b. ( ) cooks on a portable stove
    c. ( ) calls a restaurant to deliver

2. The cheeseburgers tide him over until about 3:00 P.M.

    a. ( ) make (him) hungrier
    b. ( ) help (him) survive a short period of time
    c. ( ) make (him) thirsty for a short period of time

3. George says he wants to do without food like cheeseburgers, but can't.

    a. ( ) live, survive not having
    b. ( ) eat
    c. ( ) go to a coffee shop for

4. Every day George <u>polishes off</u> two more cheeseburgers.

    a. ( ) calls his favorite restaurant for
    b. ( ) takes a small bite of
    c. ( ) finishes eating completely

5. George won't stop eating cheeseburgers. He's <u>obsessed with</u> beef.

    a. ( ) thinks about all the time
    b. ( ) is allergic to
    c. ( ) doesn't like very much

6. Sometimes, George <u>mixes</u> mayonnaise <u>with</u> mustard and puts it on his food.

    a. ( ) confuses
    b. ( ) combines
    c. ( ) buys

7. The way George eats, he probably <u>takes in</u> about 5000 calories a day.

    a. ( ) wants
    b. ( ) needs, desires
    c. ( ) consumes

8. George tried a diet once, but he <u>stuck to</u> it for only one day — actually, for only one meal.

    a. ( ) continued to work hard at
    b. ( ) liked, enjoyed, had fun with
    c. ( ) hated

B. What Does It Go With?

DIRECTIONS: Two of the three choices after each sentence can be correctly used with the idiom. Mark the **two** correct answers.

1. Henry gulped down _____ and then ordered another one.

    a. (**x**) a chocolate milkshake

   b. (**x**) a slice of pizza
   c. (   ) the menu
Hint: The object must be food, especially a large amount of food or drink.

2. Doris says ———————————— will tide her over until dinner.

   a. (   ) a piece of fruit
   b. (   ) two candy bars
   c. (   ) a good book
Hint: The subject is usually food or drink.

3. Can you do without ———————————— for one week?

   a. (   ) television
   b. (   ) a postcard
   c. (   ) coffee
Hint: The object must be something you think you need regularly.

4. Robert polished off ———————————— in about two seconds.

   a. (   ) a double cheeseburger
   b. (   ) a big bowl of soup
   c. (   ) a diet book
Hint: The object must be food or drink.

5. Janice is obsessed with ————————————.

   a. (   ) losing weight
   b. (   ) paper
   c. (   ) movie stars
Hint: The object must be something or someone considered important.

6. Meal replacements are easy to prepare. You just mix them with ————————————.

   a. (   ) water
   b. (   ) milk
   c. (   ) the container
Hint: The object must be food or drink.

7. You'll never lose weight if you take in _____ every day.

     a.   (   ) 3,000 calories
     b.   (   ) foods high in fat
     c.   (   ) a new diet book
     Hint: The object must be food, drink, or the calories in food or drink.

8. The only way to succeed is to stick to _____ .

     a.   (   ) your diet doctor
     b.   (   ) low calorie foods
     c.   (   ) your diet and exercise plan
     Hint: The object must be food, a plan, or a project, not a person.

C.   Look It Up

DIRECTIONS: Create your own minidictionary. For each idiom, write the *meaning*, an appropriate *subject*, a *direct object* or *object of the preposition* where indicated, and an *example sentence*. If you need help, refer to the other exercises in this section. Notice the stress (/) for each idiom, the position of the pronoun object [   ], and any special grammar or stylistic notes.

When you have created your minidictionary for each chapter, you can look an idiom up whenever you need to.

1. gulp [   ] down

     Meaning: **swallow (a large amount of food**

                    or drink) quickly

     Stylistic note: **informal**
     Subject: **the salesman**
     Direct object: **his lunch**
     Example sentence: **The salesman gulped down his lunch**

                    in less than five minutes.

2. tide [   ] over

     Meaning: _____
     Stylistic note: **informal**

Subject: _____

Direct object: _____

Example sentence: _____

3. do′ without′ [   ]

Meaning: _____

Subject: _____

Object of preposition: _____

Example sentence: _____

4. po′lish [   ] off′

Meaning: _____

Stylistic note: __informal_____

Subject: _____

Direct object: _____

Example sentence: _____

5. be obsessed′ with [   ]

Meaning: _____

Subject: _____

Object of preposition: _____

Example sentence: _____

6. mix′ [   ] with [   ]

Meaning: _____

Subject: _____

Direct object: _____

Object of preposition: _____

Example sentence: _____

7. take′ in′ [   ]

Meaning: _____

Grammar note: __object is usually a noun, not a pronoun__

Subject: _____

Direct object: _____

Example sentence: _____

8. stick to [ ]

Meaning: _____

Subject: _____

Object of preposition: _____

Example sentence: _____

III. GRAMMAR EXERCISES

A. Fill It In: Prepositions and Particles

DIRECTIONS: Fill in the blanks with the correct prepositions or particles. Then play the tape and check your answers.

Andy went to a diet clinic today because he wants to lose weight.

The first thing he was asked to do was to describe the way he eats.

This is what he said:

"To tell you the truth, I gulp   **down**   every meal. I polish
                                    1

_____ breakfast in one minue, lunch in two minutes, and din-
          2

ner in three minutes. An hour after dinner, I get hungry again and eat

some ice cream. I like to mix vanilla   _____   chocolate. But
                                          3

that doesn't tide me   _____   until breakfast; I usually eat some
                          4

cookies before I go to sleep.

"I know I take   _____   too many calories a day, but what
                    5

can I do? I'm obsessed   _____   food. I've tried many different
                            6

diets, but I can't do _____ soda and sweets, so I can't stick
                             7

_____ any diet for more than one day."
        8

The counselor hypnotized Andy and told him he would never

want to eat sweets again. Andy went home and ate a dish of ice cream.

B.   Fill It In: Object Pronouns

DIRECTIONS: In each sentence, fill in *one* of the blanks with the object
pronoun in parentheses.

1.   It's much better for your health to eat your food slowly and to

chew it completely instead of gulping ___**it**___ down
                                             a

_____! (it)
        b

2.   Have an apple. It'll tide _____ over _____
                                      a   b

(you) until dinner.

3.   You drink too much soda. Can't you do _____ without
                                                  a

_____? (it)
        b

4.   Where's the ice cream? Don't tell me you polished

_____ off _____! (it)
        a   b

5.   All he talks about are his muscles. I think he's obsessed

_____ with _____.   (them)
        a   b

6.   To make salad dressing, start with a small amount of oil. Then

mix _____ three times as much vinegar with
           a

_____. (it)
        b

7. That diet works very well if you stick _____ to
   _a

_____ . (it)
_b

IV. LISTENING COMPREHENSION EXERCISE

A. Listen In

DIRECTIONS: You will hear a situation presented in one or two sentences. Listen to each situation and mark the response here that most closely corresponds to the situation.

1. a. ( ) The doctor said not to eat anything between meals.
   b. (**x**) Don should eat vegetables to help him survive the time between meals.
   c. ( ) Don has to eat carrots and celery for lunch and dinner.

2. a. ( ) Many doctors eat egg yolks.
   b. ( ) Many doctors recommend eggs for dieters.
   c. ( ) Many doctors think their patients should not eat eggs every day.

3. a. ( ) To lose weight and stay thin you need to eat right and exercise for the rest of your life.
   b. ( ) The only way to lose weight is to do it quickly.
   c. ( ) It isn't necessary to continue on a diet forever.

4. a. ( ) If you're still hungry after a meal, eat more.
   b. ( ) If you eat quickly, you're probably not hungry when you finish.
   c. ( ) If you eat quickly, you're probably still hungry when you finish.

5. a. ( ) To reduce stress, sit in a quiet, comfortable place and try not to breathe.
   b. ( ) Slowly breathing in and out helps reduce stress.
   c. ( ) It's impossible to reduce stress.

6.   a.   (   ) Never put apples or raisins in your cottage cheese.

     b.   (   ) It's better to eat cottage cheese and yogurt separately.

     c.   (   ) Cottage cheese can be combined with yogurt, apples, raisins, and walnuts.

7.   a.   (   ) Linda hates exercise, but she does it anyway.

     b.   (   ) Linda doesn't exercise every day.

     c.   (   ) Linda thinks about exercise all the time.

8.   a.   (   ) Bob never drinks more than one beer.

     b.   (   ) Bob finishes five or six beers when he says he wants only one.

     c.   (   ) Bob can't finish five or six cans of beer.

V. WRITING EXERCISE

A. Finish It Up

DIRECTIONS: Finish this entry in your diary. Use as many idioms as you can.

Dear Diary,

    I started a new diet today. Instead of polishing off a box of cookies this afternoon, I ate two carrots. It's amazing,

VI. CONVERSATION ACTIVITIES

A. Act It Out

> DIRECTIONS: Read each of the following situations and act it out. Use as many idioms as possible. Work with a partner.

1. It's your first day at a diet clinic. One of the counselors asks you to describe how and what you eat for breakfast, lunch, and dinner, and for snacks. Answer the counselor's questions. For example, say, "I usually gulp down . . ."

2. You're a counselor at a diet club. A dieter tells you he's been on a diet for two weeks but hasn't lost any weight. Now he wants to try diet pills because, if he doesn't lose weight soon, he's going to return to his old ways of eating. Give him advice.

3. You're 80 pounds overweight and you've tried many ways to lose weight, but nothing has worked. Recently, you read about the Gastric Bubble, a plastic balloon that can be placed in the stomach to make you feel full. With the Gastric Bubble, you follow a low-calorie diet and you can lose a lot of weight. You want to try this new technique. Discuss it with a friend.

B. Talk It Over

1. Move around the room and find a classmate who . . .   Write his or her name here.

   a. gulps down a cup of coffee for breakfast every morning.   _____

   b. can polish off a loaf of bread.   _____

   c. can do without dessert.   _____

   d. eats fruit to tide him or her over between lunch and dinner.   _____

   e. is obsessed with cigarettes.   _____

   f. has tried a diet powder mixed with milk.   _____

g. takes in less than 1300 calories a
 day.

 _____

h. went on a diet but couldn't stick
 to it.

 _____

2. DIRECTIONS: Match the helpful hints with the dieter's problem.
 Work with a partner.

The Dieter's Problem	Helpful Hints
_____ 1. I gulp down every meal.	a. Taste the food but don't swallow it.
_____ 2. I eat salty nuts to tide me over between meals.	b. Count your calories after each meal.
	c. Carry a bag of vegetables and eat them when you get hungry.
_____ 3. I have no idea how many calories I take in every day.	
	d. Drink at least eight glasses of water a day.
_____ 4. I want to do without candy, but I can't.	e. If you go off your diet, start again the next day.
_____ 5. While I'm cooking, I polish off half the food.	f. Read the newspaper while you eat to help you eat slower.
_____ 6. I'm obsessed with food, so I always eat too fast.	g. Put your fork down after each bite.
_____ 7. I lost 12 pounds on a low-calorie diet, but I didn't stick to it.	h. Imagine yourself thinner and see that picture when you want something sweet.
_____ 8. When I'm thirsty, I mix cocoa with milk.	

Now list the three Helpful Hints you think are the most helpful.

1. _____

2. _____

3. _____

REVIEW I: MIX THEM UP

WARM-UP EXERCISE

Form groups of four or five students. Each member of the group should list his or her three favorite idioms:

1. _____

2. _____

3. _____

Together, write a sentence using one or two of the idioms your group selected. The message should be positive or funny. Next, write the sentence on a poster and decorate the poster. Hang the poster on the wall of your classroom. For example:

> *Take care of me, and I'll take care of you!*
> ♡　♡　♡　♡　♡　♡　♡

These are the thirty-one idioms in Chapters 1 to 5:

be good at	focus on	polish off
be obsessed with	get in touch with	root for
be on the phone	get through	sign up for
bring up	give birth to	stand out
call up	go for	stick to
compete against	grow up	take care of
do without	gulp down	take in
drop out	hang up	tell apart
figure out	keep in touch with	tide over
fill out	keep up with	work on
	mix with	

I. MATCH THEM UP

In addition to the idioms presented in each chapter, you have been learning idioms from the titles of the exercises in this book. Let's see if you know what they mean.

DIRECTIONS: Match the idioms on the left with the meanings on the right.

__c__ 1. Get the picture?

_____ 2. Figure it out.[1]

_____ 3. What does it go with?

_____ 4. Look it up.

_____ 5. Fill it in.

_____ 6. Listen in.

_____ 7. Finish it up.

_____ 8. Act it out.

_____ 9. Talk it over.

a. perform; pretend

b. pay attention to a conversation

c. understand

d. write the answers in the blank spaces

e. match; fit together with

f. try to understand something that may be difficult

g. complete something already started

h. try to find in a dictionary or list

i. discuss; share information

II. MIX THEM UP

DIRECTIONS: Mark the answer that completes each sentence correctly.

1. Harvey didn't want to go to school because he couldn't

_____ his class.

a. (   ) keep in touch with
b. (x) keep up with

1. This idiom is also presented in Chapter 4, *Education*.

2.   Jeanne has been playing the guitar for ten years. She

_____.

   a.   ( ) is on the phone
   b.   ( ) is good at it

3.   How many calories do you _____ each day?

   a.   ( ) take in
   b.   ( ) take care of

4.   Annette talks about surfing all the time. She _____ it.

   a.   ( ) is on the phone
   b.   ( ) is obsessed with

III.   LOOK FOR IT: IDIOMS WITH "UP"

DIRECTIONS: Find all the words in the puzzle and circle them. Each one is part of an idiom with "up." The first answer is circled for you.

T	I	Y	D	H	G	N	R
K	N	O	C	A	L	L	V
L	S	I	G	N	B	O	F
J	C	Z	F	G	R	E	W
X	A	B	M	P	I	Q	H
K	E	E	P	I	N	G	C
B	A	Z	L	O	G	Y	J

1. to telephone = to __**call**__ up.

2. When you finish a telephone conversation, you _____ up.

3. Jessica was born in Oklahoma, but she _____ up in Texas.

4. Where do you want to _____ up your children: in the city or in the country?

5. If you want to play on the soccer team, you have to _____ up for it in the Physical Education Office.

6. Don is such a good runner, he didn't have any trouble _____ up with the other runners in the race.

IV. FIND OUT: IDIOMS WITH "OUT"

DIRECTIONS: Rewrite the following paragraph using idioms with "out." Look at the list on page 74 if necessary. Pay attention to verb tenses.

When Dennis was in high school, he (was noticeable)[1] as one of the smartest students in his class. He applied to some of the best universities in the country. He (completed)[2] many application forms and was accepted by every school he applied to.

He decided to go to Yale. On his first day at college, he couldn't (understand)[3] the map of the school buildings, and he spent an hour looking for the science building. When he saw that there were 200 students in his chemistry class, he decided to find a smaller school. On the second day of classes he (stopped attending)[4].

___**When Dennis was in high school, he stood out as one of the**___

smartest students in his class.

_____

_____

_____

_____

_____

_____

_____

V. FILL IT IN: IDIOMS WITH "WITH"

DIRECTIONS: Fill in the blanks with the correct verbs. Each one is part of an idiom with "with."

Philip is ___obsessed___ with learning English. Ten
                    1

years after graduating from high school, he _____ in
                                              2

touch with his English teacher. He wrote her a letter saying he wanted

to _____ in touch with her to practice his English. He
     3

said he needed to practice with a native speaker of English or he would

_____ his own language with English, and he didn't want
     4

that to happen.

His teacher wrote back and said she could _____
                                            5

without this correspondence. Poor Philip was disappointed.

VI. DO IT OVER

DIRECTIONS: Rewrite the following story using twelve idioms from the list on page 74.

Joseph decided to (telephone) his ex-wife in London on her birthday. But each time he tried to (contact) her, he couldn't (reach her). He would (put down the receiver) and try again. On her birthday, she (talked on the telephone) all day.

Between calls, Joseph (quickly swallowed) a few glasses of wine and soon (completely finished) the bottle. He knew her line would be busy for hours, but he had decided to wish his ex-wife a happy birthday, and he intended to (continue to work hard at) his decision.

By the time his ex-wife answered, Joseph was completely drunk and his poor ex-wife couldn't (understand) what he was saying. She accused him of (thinking about liquor all the time) and told him not to try to (have regular contact with) her.

Joseph decided to call up his ex-wife in London on her birthday.

VII. FILL IT IN: CROSSWORD PUZZLE

Across

4. The twins look so similar, nobody can tell them _____.
5. The line is busy. Somebody is on the _____.
7. You're _____ with sports.
9. To have a baby boy means to give _____ to a baby boy.
11. He _____ out of school last year.
12. Take _____ of yourself!
13. How long have you been _____ on your English?
14. You should try to ___ without dessert.
16. When you end a telephone conversation, you _____ up.
18. To understand means to _____ out.
20. To try to win means to go ____ it.

Down

1. It isn't easy to _____ up with the more advanced runners in the group.
2. He's an excellent basketball player. He really _____ out.
3. Don't forget to keep in _____ with us.
6. An apple will _____ you over between lunch and dinner.
8. Where were you _____ up?
10. To reach somebody by telephone means to get _____.
15. To eat quickly means to polish _____.
17. Did you chew your food or did you _____ it down?
19. To support means to _____ for.

80

6 PERSISTENCE

WARM-UP EXERCISE

Complete these sentences. Then share them with your group or class.

One thing I want to do in my life is _____

_____

I wish I could _____

I feel good when I _____

READING SELECTION

DIRECTIONS: Read the following story silently. Then do the reading exercises that follow.

Don't Give Up

It sounds like a dream. It must be a dream: An international language that has only sixteen grammar rules and no exceptions, words spelled the way they're pronounced, and regular stress. Well, it's not a dream. There is such a language. It's called "Esperanto." And the best thing about it is that it can be learned in only three months.

In 1887, Ludovic Zamenhof, a Polish eye doctor, developed Esperanto. He wanted to make it a second language for people all over the world.

Dr. Zamenhof wrote several books under the pen name[1] "Doktoro Esperanto." He translated the Old Testament and some of the works of great writers like Shakespeare, Molière, and Gogol into Esperanto.

Today, more than 30,000 books (mostly translations) have been published[2] in Esperanto. The organization of Esperanto supporters, *Universala Esperanto-Asocio*, has members in over eighty countries. These Esperantists have been **keeping up** the work of Zamenhof, but the language still hasn't **caught on.**

Esperantists, however, are hopeful. They think they **stand a chance of** pesuading the United Nations (U.N.) to make Esperanto its official language. The U.N. has already **turned down** their proposal, but the Esperantists will not **give up.** They believe that, some day, they will **win out.**

Will the Esperantists ever **pull** it **off?** Probably not. The language **is up against** some real competition. The biggest competitor has many more grammar rules than sixteen; it has many exceptions to the rules; its words are spelled very differently from the way they're pronounced; and stress is not very regular. Also, anyone reading this story knows that it certainly cannot be learned in three months. The language? La angla,[3] of course!

---

1. A name used by an author instead of the author's true name.
2. Printed to sell to the public.
3. "La angla" is Esperanto for "English."

I. READING EXERCISES

A. Get the Picture? Comprehension

DIRECTIONS: The following questions are based on the story you just read. Write "True" or "False" after each statement.

1. Members of *Universala Esperanto-Asocio* continue the work Zamenhof started.   **True**

2. Esperanto has become very popular.   _____

3. The Esperantists still think there's a possibility of making Esperanto the official language of the U.N.   _____

4. The United Nations said "no" to the Esperantists' proposal to make Esperanto the official language of the U.N.   _____

5. The Esperantists stopped trying to make Esperanto the official language of the U.N.   _____

6. Esperantists think they will succeed someday.   _____

7. Esperanto doesn't have any competition.   _____

B. Get the Picture? Inferences

DIRECTIONS: An inference is something that is not stated directly, but is implied. Write "True" or "False" after each inference.

1. Esperanto is a much harder language to learn than English.   _____

2. Members of *Universala Esperanto-Asocio* translate works into Esperanto and teach Esperanto all over the world.   _____

3. When Zamenhof developed Esperanto, he made it as simple as possible.   _____

C. Get the Picture? Main Idea

DIRECTIONS: Mark the one statement that represents the main idea of the story.

1. ( ) Ludovic Zamenhof developed a simple language called "Esperanto" and translated many books into this language.

2. (   ) The United Nations did not want to make Esperanto its official language.

3. (   ) Zamenhof and his followers tried to make Esperanto popular, but the language still hasn't been accepted around the world.

II. MEANING EXERCISES

A. Figure It Out

DIRECTIONS: Mark the meaning of the idiom underlined in each sentence.

1. Xavier Roberts, a sculptor, designed the models for simple, ugly dolls called "Cabbage Patch Kids." Some companies thought a funny-looking doll didn't <u>stand a chance of</u> selling well.

    a. (   ) seem to be modern enough for
    b. (   ) need any help
    c. (**x**) have a good possibility of

2. Roberts's agents weren't worried. They <u>kept up</u> their plan to make these dolls a success.

    a. (,) continued
    b. (   ) stopped
    c. (   ) discussed

3. After two companies <u>turned</u> them <u>down</u>, Roberts's agents went to a company called Coleco Industries.

    a. (   ) insulted (them)
    b. (,) rejected (their request)
    c. (   ) accepted (their request)

4. The agents didn't want to <u>give up</u>.

    a. (   ) sell the idea, negotiate a deal
    b. (   ) give the dolls to the company for free
    c. (,) stop trying, abandon something

5. They told Coleco Industries about their dolls, which all had birth certificates and adoption papers, and they finally <u>won out</u>.

    a. (,) were successful in the end
    b. (   ) presented their idea unsuccessfully
    c. (   ) stopped trying

6. Everyone was surprised that they <u>pulled</u> it <u>off</u>.

      a. ( ) removed the head
      b. (✓) were successful at something difficult
      c. ( ) weren't successful at something difficult

7. The first year they were in the stores, the Cabbage Patch dolls <u>were up against</u> a lot of competition.

      a. (✓) had to deal with
      b. ( ) needed
      c. ( ) didn't need

8. The dolls <u>caught on</u> for many reasons. Some say the reason was because they were so ugly. Others say it was because each doll was different. And some believe it was because of the adoption papers.

      a. ( ) were cute
      b. ( ) didn't sell very well
      c. (✓) became popular

B. What Does It Go With?

DIRECTIONS: Two of the three choices after each sentence can be correctly used with the idiom. Mark the *two* correct answers.

1. To lose weight, you have to keep up _____.

      a. (x) your exercises
      b. (x) your diet
      c. ( ) last night's dinner
      Hint: The object must be something that can be continued.

2. In the 1980s, _____ caught on in the United States.

      a. ( ) videocassette recorders
      b. ( ) personal computers
      c. ( ) fires
      Hint: The subject must be something that can be popular.

3. That movie doesn't stand a chance of _____.

    a. ( ) becoming popular
    b. ( ) its director
    c. ( ) winning an Academy Award
    Hint: The object must represent something difficult.

4. The company turned down _____.

    a. ( ) his typing
    b. ( ) his job application
    c. ( ) Patrick
    Hint: The object must be a person or a request.

5. _____ gave up after trying several ways to save his life.

    a. ( ) The ambulance
    b. ( ) The team of doctors
    c. ( ) His wife
    Hint: The subject must be a person or persons.

6. Although it was difficult, the _____ finally won out.

    a. ( ) union representatives
    b. ( ) revolutionaries
    c. ( ) sickness
    Hint: The subject must be a person or persons.

7. Nobody believed the Democrats could pull off

    _____.

    a. ( ) the election
    b. ( ) their candidate
    c. ( ) such a big victory
    Hint: The object must be something that represents success, not a person.

8. The President is up against _____.

    a. ( ) an impossible situation
    b. ( ) the voters
    c. ( ) a strong candidate
    Hint: The object must represent a difficulty or competition.

C. Look It Up

DIRECTIONS: Create your own minidictionary. For each idiom, write the *meaning*, an appropriate *subject*, a *direct object* or *object of the preposition* where indicated, and an *example sentence*. If you need help, refer to the other exercises in this section. Notice the stress (/) for each idiom, the position of the pronoun object [   ], and any special grammar or stylistic notes.

When you have created your minidictionary for each chapter, you can look an idiom up whenever you need to.

1. keep [   ] up

    Meaning: __continue__

    Grammar notes: __usually the imperative form;__

    __the object is often "it"__

    Subject: __his followers__

    Direct object: __his work__

    Example sentence: __His followers kept up his work for__

    __many years.__

2. catch on

    Meaning: _____

    Stylistic note: __informal__

    Subject: _____

    Example sentence: _____

3. stand a chance, stand a chance of [   ]

    Meaning: _____

    Grammar note: __object of the preposition is usually__

    __the -ing form__

    Subject: _____

    Object of preposition: _____

    Example sentence: _____

4. turn [   ] down

    Meaning: _____

    Subject: _____

Direct object: _____

Example sentence: _____

5. give up, give [   ] up

Meaning: _____

Subject: _____

Direct object: _____

Example sentence: _____

6. win out

Meaning: _____

Stylistic note: __informal_____

Subject: _____

Example sentence: _____

7. pull [   ] off

Meaning: _____

Stylistic note: __informal_____

Subject: _____

Direct object: _____

Example sentence: _____

8. be up against [   ]

Meaning: _____

Stylistic note: __informal_____

Subject: _____

Object of preposition: _____

Example sentence: _____

III.   GRAMMAR EXERCISES

A.   Fill It In: Prepositions and Particles

DIRECTIONS: Fill in the blanks with the correct prepositions or particles. Then play the tape and check your answers.

Bruce wanted to be a baseball player, but everybody told him he

didn't stand a chance ____of____ getting on the team. Bruce prac-
                          1
ticed every day. He kept _____ the practice for months and
                              2
never gave _____. He was sure he would pull it
               3
_____ although he was _____ _____ a lot
     4   5   6
of competition.

Unfortunately, Bruce didn't win _____. He was turned
                                      7
_____ because he was too young. The minimum age was nine.
     8

B.   Fill It In: Object Pronouns

DIRECTIONS: In each sentence, fill in *one* of the blanks with the object pronoun in parentheses.

1. L. Sauveur and M. Berlitz developed the "Direct Method" of learn-

    ing a language, and their followers kept ____it____ up
                                                  a

    _____. (it)
         b

2. The first time Tom applied for a visa, the Consulate turned

    _____ down _____. (him)
         a   b

3. In the movie, a 25-year-old actor played the part of an 80-year-
    old man. Nobody could believe how well he pulled

    _____ off _____. (it)
         a   b

IV.   LISTENING COMPREHENSION EXERCISE

A.   Listen In

DIRECTIONS: You will hear a situation presented in one or two sentences. Listen to each situation and mark the response here that most closely corresponds to the situation.

1. a. (   ) Charles ran quickly the whole way.
    b. (**x**) Charles started fast but got slower and didn't finish.
    c. (   ) Charles started slowly and then ran faster.

2. a. ( ) Americans love music from other countries.
   b. ( ) If the music is good, a song will be popular in the United States.
   c. ( ) If the words are in English, a song from another country can become popular in the United States.

3. a. ( ) Elaine is not a good student.
   b. ( ) Elaine has a good possibility of getting a Ph.D.
   c. ( ) There's no possibility that Elaine will get a Ph.D.

4. a. ( ) Mark joined the army.
   b. ( ) Mark is a doctor.
   c. ( ) The Army didn't accept Mark because of medical reasons.

5. a. ( ) The hockey team will not stop trying to win.
   b. ( ) The hockey team never loses.
   c. ( ) Their score is going up.

6. a. ( ) Pierre's parents want him to stay in the United States.
   b. ( ) Pierre's parents are in the United States.
   c. ( ) Pierre wants to stay in the United States and believes he will succeed in the end.

7. a. ( ) It was difficult, but David lost the weight.
   b. ( ) David gained 30 pounds to be in the Olympics.
   c. ( ) David's coach lost 30 pounds.

8. a. ( ) Jennifer is the best student at Harvard.
   b. ( ) Jennifer has a lot of competition at Harvard.
   c. ( ) Jennifer doesn't like the smartest students at Harvard.

V. WRITING EXERCISE

A. Finish It Up

DIRECTIONS: Finish this entry in your diary. Use as many idioms as you can.

Dear Diary,
    I'm so excited! I can't
believe I pulled it off. Today,
I heard that

VI.　CONVERSATION EXERCISES

A.　Act It Out

> DIRECTIONS: Read each of the following situations and act it out. Use as many idioms as possible. Work with a partner.

be up against	keep up	stand a chance of
catch on	pull off	turn down
give up		win out

1. You're the parents of a high school girl who wants to go to one of the Ivy League[4] schools to study economics. Today, she got a rejection from Yale. Discuss the situation. For example, say, "Don't give up, honey. You . . ."

2. You are a young actor who just finished acting school, and you are looking for your first job in the theater. You just came back from an audition, and you are discussing your chances of getting the part with your roommate, an engineer.

3. You're the vice president of a small, but very successful, toy company. Your boss, the president, is thinking about retiring. You want to become president, but several other senior employees do, too. Discuss your plan for getting the job with your wife/husband/best friend.

B.　Talk It Over

Move around the room and find a class-mate who . . .

Write his or her name here.

a. was up against a lot of competition in school.

　　＿＿＿＿＿＿＿＿＿＿＿＿

　　Which school?

　　＿＿＿＿＿＿＿＿＿＿＿＿

4. Harvard University, Yale University, University of Pennsylvania, Princeton University, Columbia University, Brown University, Dartmouth College, and Cornell University.

b. wanted to marry someone but was turned down.

    _____

c. thinks he or she doesn't stand a chance of learning to speak English fluently.

    _____

d. started a sport when he or she was young and kept it up.

    _____

Which sport?

    _____

e. wants to be very famous and thinks he or she will pull it off.

    _____

f. wanted to get a university degree but gave up.

    _____

g. is interested in a field that is just beginning to catch on.

    _____

Which field?

    _____

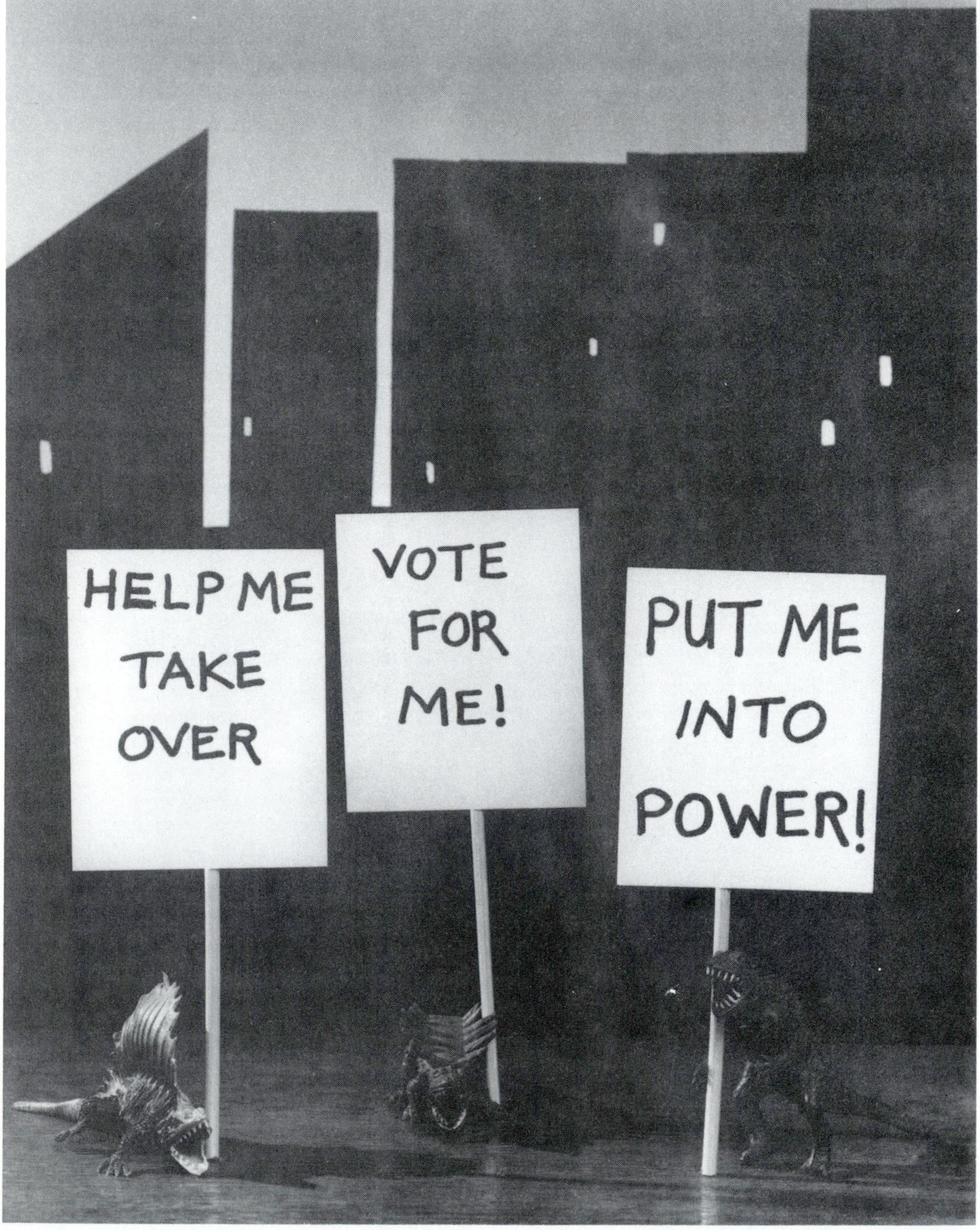
HELP ME
TAKE
OVER
VOTE
FOR
ME!
PUT ME
INTO
POWER!

7 POLITICS

WARM-UP EXERCISES

Describe the ideal politician — for example, mayor, governor, or president. Write three adjectives below.

The ideal politician is _____

_____

_____

Share your answers with the class.

If you were a politician, what would you change in the United States?

_____

READING SELECTION

DIRECTIONS: Read the following story silently. Then do the reading exercises that follow.

Vote for Me

In 1984, Geraldine Ferraro of Queens, New York, became the first woman to **run for** vice president of the United States. Before the election,[1] Ferraro traveled across the country with Walter Mondale, who hoped to become president. Mondale and Ferraro asked Americans in every state to **vote for** them.

But on January 20, 1985, the Mondale – Ferraro team[2] wasn't **sworn in.** The American voters didn't **put** a woman **into power.** In fact, only Mondale's home state of Minnesota and the District of Columbia voted for the Democrats, so the Republicans **took over** the White House once again.

What happened? Did the voters **disapprove of** Mondale or **were** they **against** Ferraro? Did they have questions about Ferraro's family's money, her husband's business connections, or her position supporting abortion?[3] Or were President Reagan and Vice President Bush just too popular?

No one really knows why Mondale and Ferraro didn't win, but we do know that by trying to become vice president, Ferraro **paved the way for** other women in national politics.

1. Opportunity to support a candidate by vote.
2. People on the same side in a contest.
3. Stopping a pregnancy by forcing a fetus from the mother's womb.

I. READING EXERCISES

A. Get the Picture? Comprehension

DIRECTIONS: These questions are based on the story you just read. Write "True" or "False" after each statement.

1. Ferraro wanted to be vice president but didn't try to be elected.   **False**

2. Ferraro wanted Americans to support her and Mondale on Election Day.   _____

3. Mondale and Ferraro promised to accept the responsibilities of president and vice president in a ceremony on January 20, 1985.   _____

4. The voters didn't make Ferraro vice president.   _____

5. The Democrats became the leaders of the country again.   _____

6. Some people wondered whether the voters didn't like Mondale.   _____

7. They also asked if the voters didn't like Ferraro.   _____

8. Ferraro's attempt to become vice president made it harder for other women to enter national politics.   _____

B. Get the Picture? Inferences

DIRECTIONS: An inference is something that is not stated directly, but is implied. Write "True" or "False" after each inference.

1. There was no information about Ferraro's personal life during the campaign.   _____

2. Women had run in presidential elections in the United States before Ferraro tried to become vice president.   _____

3. Having Ferraro as the vice presidential candidate didn't help Walter Mondale become president. _____

C. Get the Picture? Main Idea

DIRECTIONS: Mark the one statement that represents the main idea of the story.

1. ( ) She wasn't elected, but Geraldine Ferraro did something important by trying to become vice president in the 1984 national election.

2. ( ) It's impossible for a woman to be elected to a high government position in the United States.

3. ( ) The Reagan-Bush team was elected in 1980 and then re-elected in 1984, beating Mondale and Ferraro.

II. MEANING EXERCISES

A. Figure It Out

DIRECTIONS: Mark the meaning of the idiom underlined in each sentence.

1. In 1984, Jesse Jackson became the first black to run for president of the United States.

   a. ( ) like the
   b. ( ) debate the
   c. (x) become a candidate for

2. But the American people didn't have a chance to vote for Jackson because he wasn't nominated by the Democratic party.

   a. ( ) support by ballot (in an election)
   b. ( ) consider (in an election)
   c. ( ) see

3. So, he couldn't be elected and <u>sworn in</u> as president.

    a. ( ) cursed
    b. ( ) presented with an award for being
    c. ( ) asked to promise to perform the duties of office

4. That year, Ronald Reagan was <u>put into power</u> for the second time.

    a. ( ) considered a powerful candidate
    b. ( ) given political control through an election
    c. ( ) trying to become president of the country

5. The Democrats didn't <u>take over</u> the White House.

    a. ( ) take control of
    b. ( ) change
    c. ( ) want control of

6. Many people <u>disapproved of</u> Reagan's foreign policies, but they elected him anyway.

    a. ( ) didn't know about
    b. ( ) weren't sure of
    c. ( ) were against

7. Some people said they voted for Reagan, not because they liked him, but because they <u>were against</u> Mondale and Ferraro

    a. ( ) opposed
    b. ( ) wanted
    c. ( ) didn't know

8. Jackson didn't get elected. He didn't even get his party's nomination. But he did <u>pave the way for</u> other minorities[4] to run in national elections.

    a. ( ) make it possible for
    b. ( ) make it impossible for
    c. ( ) want

4. A racial, religious, or political group smaller than the group that is in control.

B.   What Does It Go With?

DIRECTIONS: Two of the three choices after each sentence can be correctly used with the idiom. Mark the *two* correct answers.

1.   It's hard to believe he's going to run for _____ again.

      a.   ( ) the Democrats
      b.   (x) office
      c.   (x) president
      Hint: The object must represent a political position.

2.   Which _____ are you going to vote for?

      a.   ( ) candidate
      b.   ( ) political party
      c.   ( ) election
      Hint: The object must be a person or political party.

3.   A judge will swear in _____ soon.

      a.   ( ) the president of the company
      b.   ( ) the new governor
      c.   ( ) the president and vice president of the United States
      Hint: The object must be a person in a political position or a member of a club.

4.   Many Americans think the voters will not put _____ into power this election.

      a.   ( ) a woman
      b.   ( ) a Democrat
      c.   ( ) such conservative policies
      Hint: The object must be a person.

5.   If the president dies in office, _____ takes over.

      a.   ( ) the vice president
      b.   ( ) another election
      c.   ( ) the person next in line
      Hint: The subject must be a person.

6. Do you disapprove of _____?

    a. ( ) the way they're raising their children
    b. ( ) her policies
    c. ( ) the winter
    Hint: The object must be something about which you can have an opinion.

7. Joseph is against _____.

    a. ( ) a female president
    b. ( ) gambling
    c. ( ) himself
    Hint: The object must be someone or something about which you can have an opinion. The object cannot be the same as the subject.

8. Her lawsuit paved the way for _____.

    a. ( ) other women to get the same salary as men
    b. ( ) other equal-rights cases
    c. ( ) a similar case that happened a year earlier
    Hint: The object must be something that happened later.

C. Look It Up

DIRECTIONS: Create your own minidictionary. For each idiom, write the *meaning*, an appropriate *subject*, a *direct object* or *object of the preposition* where indicated, and an *example sentence*. If you need help, refer to the other exercises in this section. Notice the stress (/) for each idiom, the position of the pronoun object [ ], and any special grammar or stylistic notes.

When you have created your minidictionary for each chapter, you can look an idiom up whenever you need to.

1. run for [ ]

    Meaning: **to become a candidate for (political office)**
    Grammar note: **the object is usually a noun, not a pronoun**
    Subject: **a woman; the governor**
    Object of preposition: **president**
    Example sentence: **A woman is running for president this year.**

2. vote for [ ]
    Meaning: _____
    Subject: _____
    Object of preposition: _____
    Example sentence: _____

3. swear [ ] in
    Meaning: _____
    Grammar note: __usually passive_____
    Subject: _____
    Direct object: _____
    Example sentence: _____

4. put [ ] into power
    Meaning: _____
    Grammar note: __often passive_____
    Subject: _____
    Direct object: _____
    Example sentence: _____

5. take over, take [ ] over
    Meaning: _____
    Subject: _____
    Direct object: _____
    Example sentence: _____

6. disapprove of [ ]
    Meaning: _____
    Subject: _____
    Object of preposition: _____
    Example sentence: _____

7. be against [ ]
    Meaning: _____
    Subject: _____

Object of preposition: _____

Example sentence: _____

8. pave the way, pave the way for [ ]
   Meaning: _____
   Subject: _____
   Object of preposition: _____
   Example sentence: _____

III. GRAMMAR EXERCISES

A. Fill It In: Prepositions and Particles

DIRECTIONS: Fill in the blanks with the correct prepositions or particles. Then play the tape and check your answers.

Jimmy Carter, the governor of Georgia, became famous when he

decided to run ____**for**____ president of the United States. When
        1

he started to ask Americans to vote _____ him in the 1976
        2

campaign, voters outside his state of Georgia didn't know him. The

Republicans didn't think the voters would put Carter _____
        3

power because he had never worked in national or international politics

before. But the voters liked this young candidate who said that he

disapproved _____ the way the government was spending
        4

money. The Republicans were very surprised that the American voters

supported Carter.

Carter took _____ the presidency the year of the United
        5

States' bicentennial. Like other presidents before him, he was sworn

_____ on January 20.
   6

B. Fill It In: Object Pronouns

DIRECTIONS: In each sentence, fill in one of the blanks with the object pronoun in parentheses.

1. Laura wants to be elected to the Board of Directors. Are you going

    to vote _____ for ___**her**___? (her)
              a   b

2. Many people believe that big business supports the Republicans.

    Corporations give the money to put _____ into
             a

    _____ (them) power.
       b

3. Donald really wants to be class president. Are you going to vote

    _____ for _____? (him)
        a   b

4. In 1978, Iranians attacked the United States embassy in Teheran.

    They took _____ over _____ (it) and held
            a   b

    fifty-two Americans hostage for 14 months.

5. Jack and Margaret don't want their 17-year-old daughter to travel

    to Europe with her friends. They strongly disapprove

    _____ of _____. (it)
        a   b

6. Since Matthew lost his job, he thinks everyone is

    _____ against _____. (him)
        a   b

7. The women at the bank will be happy if Marlene becomes a vice

    president. It will pave the way _____ for
             a

    _____ (them) to get top positions at the bank too.
       b

IV. LISTENING COMPREHENSION EXERCISE

A. Listen In

DIRECTIONS: You will hear a situation presented in one or two sentences. Listen to each situation and mark the response here that most closely corresponds to the situation.

1. a. (x) Rockefeller was given the oath of office four times.

    b. ( ) Rockefeller didn't want to be governor four times.

    c. ( ) Rockefeller wasn't elected governor four times.

2. a. ( ) Most Americans think the President is doing a good job.

    b. ( ) Most Americans don't know if the President is doing a good job or not.

    c. ( ) Most Americans think the President is not doing a good job.

3. a. ( ) The President's family wants him to be a candidate in the next election.

    b. ( ) A member of the President's family wants to be a candidate for president.

    c. ( ) The President's family doesn't want him to be a candidate in the next election.

4. a. ( ) The people of Illinois supported the candidate who was born in their state.

    b. ( ) The people of Illinois didn't support the Republican candidate.

    c. ( ) The people of Illinois supported the candidate from another state.

5. a. ( ) Many voters want somebody they know to be reelected.

    b. ( ) Many voters want somebody new to be elected.

    c. ( ) Some people think the new candidate is too powerful.

1081088108   *Politics*

6. a. ( ) Ford became vice president when Nixon left office.

   b. ( ) Nixon had to become vice president.

   c. ( ) Vice President Ford became president when Nixon left office.

7. a. ( ) The Senate thinks the United States should not be involved in Central America or South America.

   b. ( ) The Senate is involved in Central America and South America.

   c. ( ) The Senate seems to support United States involvement in Central or South America.

8. a. ( ) There will never be peace in the Middle East.

   b. ( ) Peace talks make peace possible in the Middle East.

   c. ( ) Peace talks established peace in the Middle East.

V. WRITING EXERCISE

A. Finish It Up

DIRECTIONS: Finish this entry in your diary. Use as many idioms as you can.

> Dear Diary,
>   Last night I had a strange dream. I dreamed I was running for

VI. CONVERSATION ACTIVITIES

A. Act It Out

DIRECTIONS: Read each of the following situations and act it out. Use as many idioms as possible. Work with a partner.

be against	put into power	swear in
disapprove of	run for	take over
pave the way for		vote for

1. Choose a political leader you disapprove of and describe what he or she did that was so bad. Discuss it with a news reporter. For example, say, "I disapprove of . . ."

2. Describe the political situation in your own country. Who has taken over recently? Who put this person into power? How do you feel about this leader? Discuss it with an American friend who has a different opinion from yours.

3. You want to join a club. Discuss the procedure with a club member. Ask if you will be sworn in. Find out what you can do as a member.

B. Talk It Over

Move around the room and find a classmate who . . .

Write his or her name here.

a. is against nuclear weapons.   _____

b. disapproves of U.S. foreign policies.   _____

Which ones?   _____

c. would like to run for office some day.   _____

d. would vote for the death penalty if he or she could.   _____

For which crimes? _____

e. took over (or will take over) the family
    business. _____

    What kind of business? _____

f. paved the way for a younger brother
    or sister to do something. _____

    What was it? _____

g. was sworn in as a member of a club
    or organization. _____

    Which organization? _____

h. likes the person who was put into
    power in his or her city. _____

    Who was it? _____

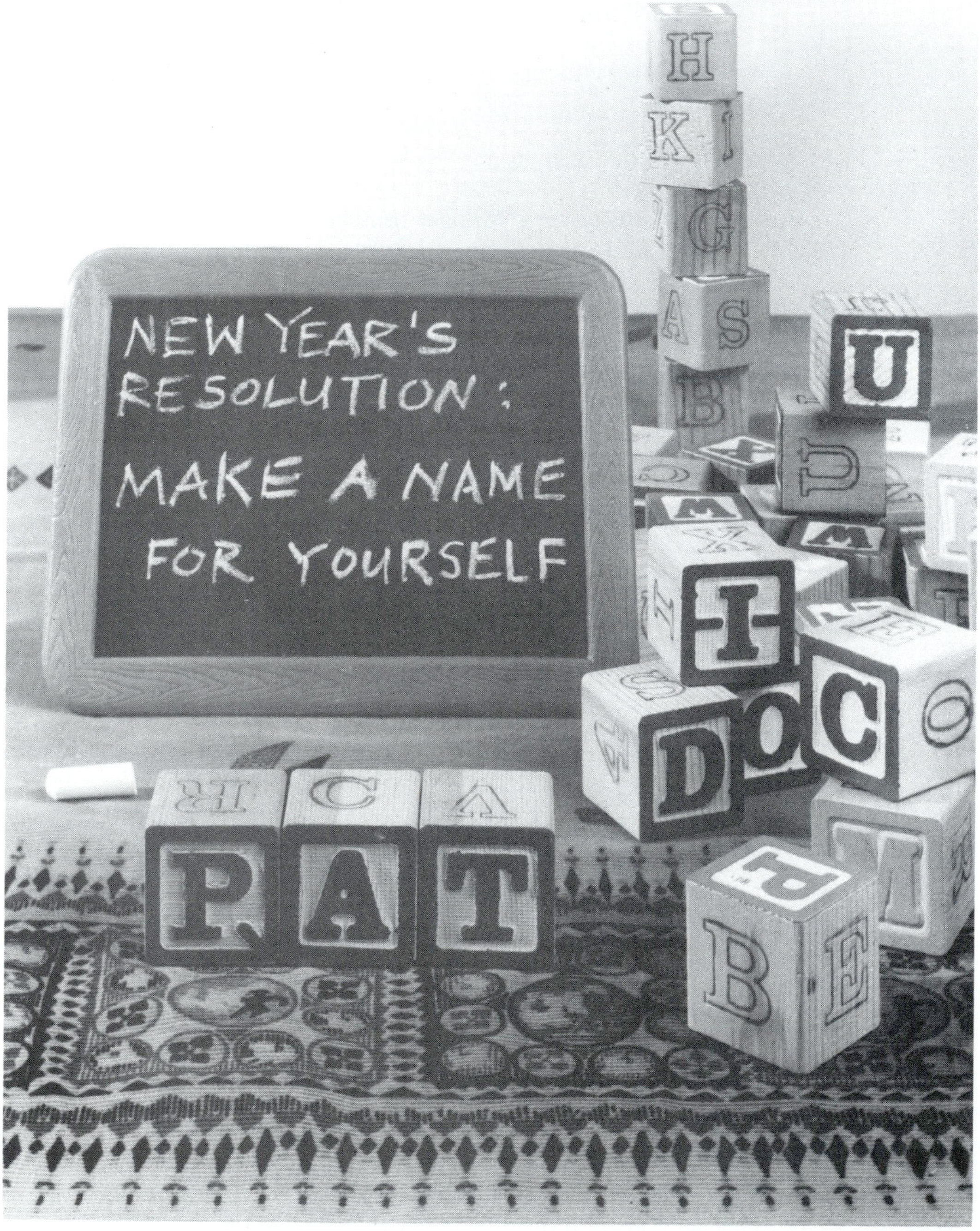
NEW YEAR'S
RESOLUTION:
MAKE A NAME
FOR YOURSELF
PAT
DOC

8 SUCCESS

WARM-UP EXERCISE

Is success important to you?   ( ) yes   ( ) no

Do you think you will be successful?   ( ) yes   ( ) no

Give three ways people become financially successful:

1. _____

2. _____

3. _____

What other kinds of success are there besides financial **success?**

1. _____

2. _____

3. _____

READING SELECTION

DIRECTIONS: Read the following story silently. Then do the reading exercises that follow.

Make a Name for Yourself

Ernest Hemingway was born in Oak Park, Illinois, in 1899. After finishing high school, he became a newspaper reporter for the *Kansas City Star*. By the time he was in his mid-20s, he had published his short stories. Then, he **got off to a good start** as a novelist with the publication of *The Sun Also Rises*. The young writer **kept on** writing and soon published *A Farewell to Arms*, which many readers said was his best work.

Hemingway **made a name for himself** not only as a writer but also as an adventurer.[1] He **took an interest in** big game[2] hunting and fishing, and he enjoyed watching bullfights. He **made use of** these experiences in his books.

When Hemingway was young, he was disappointed in love. He was **planning on** marrying a nurse he had met in World War I, but she decided to marry an Italian duke[3] instead. Hemingway was heartbroken. Later, he did get married — four times, in fact. Such events from his own life were often published in newspapers.

In 1921 Hemingway went to Paris to work as a foreign correspondent[4] for the *Toronto Star*, a Canadian newspaper. When he was there, other writers like F. Scott Fitzgerald, Gertrude Stein, and Ezra Pound **made an impression on** him.

In 1940 Hemingway's most popular novel, *For Whom the Bell Tolls*, was published. In 1953 he won the Pulitzer Prize in fiction for his novel *The Old Man and the Sea*. One year later, he won the Nobel Prize for literature. Ernest Hemingway **was destined for** greatness.

In his later years, Hemingway lived in Cuba and wrote about the country, but Castro's revolution forced him to return to the United States in 1960. The following year, his life ended with the drama of one of his novels: He killed himself with a shotgun.

---

1. A person who has exciting or dangerous experiences.
2. Large wild animals — for example, elephants or lions — hunted for sport.
3. A nobleman, lower in rank than a prince.
4. A person who goes to another country to write articles for a newspaper or magazine.

I. READING EXERCISES

A. Get the Picture? Comprehension

DIRECTIONS: These questions are based on the story you just read. Write "True" or "False" after each statement.

1. Hemingway's work as a novelist began well.   **True**

2. After publishing *The Sun Also Rises*, Hemingway stopped working hard as a novelist. _____

3. Hemingway became famous through his writing and his personal life. _____

4. He liked hunting, fishing, and going to bullfights. _____

5. Hemingway never used experiences from his own life in his novels. _____

6. Hemingway wanted to marry a nurse he met during World War I. _____

7. Other writers never influenced Hemingway. _____

8. It seemed that Hemingway was to be a great writer. _____

B. Get the Picture? Inferences

DIRECTIONS: An inference is something that is not stated directly, but is implied. Write "True" or "False" after each inference.

1. Hemingway lived a simple life. _____

2. Hemingway didn't like to travel. _____

3. Hemingway is one of the most successful twentieth-century American writers. _____

C. Get the Picture? Main Idea

DIRECTIONS: Mark the one statement that represents the main idea of the story.

1. ( ) Ernest Hemingway had a long and successful career as a writer, lived an adventurous life, and died dramatically.

2. ( ) Although he was an American, Hemingway lived in Cuba.

3. ( ) Hemingway won the Pulitzer Prize in fiction for *The Old Man and the Sea* and the Nobel Prize for literature.

II. MEANING EXERCISES

A. Figure It Out

DIRECTIONS: Mark the meaning of the idiom underlined in each sentence.

1. Jack Nicholson didn't really <u>get off to a good start</u> as an actor.

    a. (**x**) begin well
    b. ( ) get a role, act
    c. ( ) begin his career with problems

2. Nicholson <u>took an interest in</u> method acting and studied it seriously.

    a. ( ) hated, didn't want to know anything about
    b. ( ) registered for a course in
    c. ( ) wanted to know all about, was attracted to

3. Once Nicholson got a leading role, he <u>kept on</u> getting them.

    a. ( ) stopped
    b. ( ) continued
    c. ( ) didn't care about

4. Nicholson gradually <u>made a name for himself</u> through parts in the movies *One Flew Over the Cuckoo's Nest* and *Carnal Knowledge*.

    a. ( ) became famous
    b. ( ) changed his name
    c. ( ) learned to act in films

5. Nicholson <u>made</u> good <u>use of</u> what he learned in his acting classes whenever he was in a movie.

    a. ( ) used
    b. ( ) forgot
    c. ( ) didn't want to use

6. Nicholson has <u>made</u> such a strong <u>impression on</u> American movie-goers that he is often ranked with great actors of earlier periods such as Spencer Tracy and Humphrey Bogart.

    a. ( ) was considered so muscular to
    b. ( ) had an effect on
    c. ( ) was considered so funny to

7. Fortunately for movie-goers, Nicholson <u>planned on</u> making a lot of movies.

    a. ( ) got tired of
    b. ( ) was opposed to
    c. ( ) intended to

8. Jack Nicholson seemed <u>to be destined for</u> a successful acting career.

    a. ( ) was sure to have
    b. ( ) wanted
    c. ( ) worked hard to have

B. What Does It Go With?

DIRECTIONS: Two of the three choices after each sentence can be correctly used with the idiom. Mark the *two* correct answers.

1. _____ got off to a good start as a singer.

    a. ( ) That song
    b. (x) Donald
    c. (x) Barbara's sister
    Hint: The subject must be a person or persons.

2. The couple in front of us kept on _____ during the movie.

    a. ( ) taking off their coats
    b. ( ) talking
    c. ( ) eating popcorn
    Hint: The object must be an action that can continue over time.

3. _____ had made a name for herself by the time she was thirty.

    a. ( ) That fashion designer
    b. ( ) That journalist
    c. ( ) That country
    Hint: The subject must be a person.

4. Janice and Janet took an interest in _____.

    a. ( ) tomorrow
    b. ( ) running
    c. ( ) Latin dancing
    Hint: The object must be a school subject, sport, or hobby.

5. Mike doesn't know how to make use of _____.

    a. ( ) his cup of coffee
    b. ( ) his free time
    c. ( ) his new computer
    Hint: The object must be something that can be used for a purpose.

6. Billy and Marilyn have been planning on _____ for a year.

    a. ( ) changing jobs
    b. ( ) going to sleep
    c. ( ) getting married
    Hint: The object must be something important that requires thinking ahead.

7. The new doctor made an impression on _____.

    a. ( ) the hospital
    b. ( ) the rest of the hospital staff
    c. ( ) his colleagues
    Hint: The object must be a person or persons.

8. Everybody knew she was destined for _____.

    a. ( ) a successful career as a lawyer
    b. ( ) a job
    c. ( ) greatness
    Hint: The object must be something important, not something ordinary.

C. Look It Up

DIRECTIONS: Create your own minidictionary. For each idiom, write the *meaning*, an appropriate *subject*, a *direct object* or *object of the preposition* where indicated, and an *example sentence*. If you need help, refer to the other exercises in this section. Notice the stress (/) for each idiom, the position of the pronoun object [ ], and any special grammar or stylistic notes.

When you have created your minidictionary for each chapter, you can look an idiom up whenever you need to.

1. get off to a good start
    Meaning: __to begin well__
    Subject: __the new teacher, the president__
    Example sentence: __The new teacher got off to a good start in September.__

2. keep on [ ]
    Meaning: _____
    Grammar note: object is usually a gerund (the -ing form of the verb)
    Subject: _____
    Object of preposition: _____
    Example sentence: _____

3. make a name for [oneself]
    Meaning: _____
    Stylistic note: __informal__
    Subject: _____
    Object of preposition: __the reflexive__
    Example sentence: _____

4. take an interest in [ ]
    Meaning: _____
    Subject: _____
    Object of preposition: _____
    Example sentence: _____

5. máke úse of [   ]

   Meaning: _____

   Subject: _____

   Object of preposition: _____

   Example sentence: _____

6. plán on [   ]

   Meaning: _____

   Grammar note: object is often a gerund (the -ing form of

   the verb)

   Subject: _____

   Object of preposition: _____

   Example sentence: _____

7. máke an impréssion on [   ]

   Meaning: _____

   Subject: _____

   Object of preposition: _____

   Example sentence: _____

8. be déstined for [   ]

   Meaning: _____

   Subject: _____

   Object of preposition: _____

   Example sentence: _____

III. GRAMMAR EXERCISES

A. Fill It In: Prepositions and Particles

> DIRECTIONS: Fill in the blanks with the correct prepositions or particles. Then play the tape and check your answers.

Tom Jenks became famous as the man who edited a 1500-page manuscript by Ernest Hemingway into a 247-page novel called *The Garden of Eden*.

Jenks was, in fact, the fourth editor at Charles Scribner's Sons to work on *The Garden of Eden*. The three editors before him couldn't do the job, but Jenks just kept ____**on**____ making changes. He didn't

1

rewrite; he made use _____ Hemingway's own words.

2

Before starting the Hemingway book, Jenks never really took an interest _____ the great writer. Jenks was planning _____

3 4

publishing new writers at Scribner's. Maybe because he wasn't very interested in Hemingway, Jenks got _____ _____ a good

5 6

start and was able to finish the job that Hemingway himself hadn't finished.

The early reviews of the book were very negative. But like *Islands in the Stream*,[5] which sold over a million copies after bad reviews, *The Garden of Eden* was destined _____ success.

7

B. Fill It In: Object Pronouns

DIRECTIONS: In each sentence, fill in *one* of the blanks with the object pronoun in parentheses.

1. That young lawyer is so lazy, he'll never make _____
    <u>a</u>

    a name for __**himself**__. (himself)
    <u>b</u>

2. Harold   hates   swimming.   He   never   took   an   interest

    _____   in   _____. (it)
    <u>a</u>   <u>b</u>

3. Jessica has her own car but she really doesn't make use

    _____   of   _____. (it)
    <u>a</u>   <u>b</u>

4. Max didn't know he was going to see his ex-wife in Boston. He

    wasn't planning _____ on _____. (it)
    <u>a</u>   <u>b</u>

5. Ms. Tuttle, the owner of the gallery, likes the painter's work. It

    must have made a strong impression _____ on
    <u>a</u>

    _____. (her)
    <u>b</u>

6. Everyone knew John would be a famous tennis player some day.

    He was destined _____ for _____. (it)
    <u>a</u>   <u>b</u>

5. The first Hemingway novel published after the writer's death.

IV. LISTENING COMPREHENSION EXERCISE

A. Listen In

DIRECTIONS: You will hear a situation presented in one or two sentences. Listen to each situation and mark the response that most closely corresponds to the situation.

1. a. ( ) Doug is a famous comedian.
    b. (x) Doug is trying to become a famous comedian.
    c. ( ) It isn't easy for Doug to remember the name of that comedian.

2. a. ( ) George can find a way to use everything.
    b. ( ) George has a small waist.
    c. ( ) George wastes paper.

3. a. ( ) Lisa went to college in Japan.
    b. ( ) Lisa wants to learn the Japanese language.
    c. ( ) Lisa likes the Japanese people.

4. a. ( ) Tom's clothes had a good effect on his girlfriend's parents.
    b. ( ) Tom's clothes had a bad effect on his girlfriend's parents.
    c. ( ) Tom didn't go to his girlfriend's house for Thanksgiving dinner because he didn't have anything to wear.

5. a. ( ) Carol continued to gamble after losing $500.
    b. ( ) Carol stopped gambling after losing $500.
    c. ( ) Carol won $500 while gambling.

6. a. ( ) It wasn't Joan's fate to be a musician.
    b. ( ) It was Joan's fate that she would be a musician.
    c. ( ) Joan's parents didn't want their daughter to be a musician.

7. a. ( ) Anne's project went well in the beginning.
    b. ( ) Anne's project began well and ended well.
    c. ( ) Anne never began her photography project.

8. a. ( ) Jeff went to law school.
    b. ( ) Jeff didn't want to go to law school.
    c. ( ) Jeff wanted to go to law school but wasn't accepted.

V. WRITING EXERCISE

A. Finish It Up

DIRECTIONS: Finish this entry in your diary. Use as many idioms as you can.

> Dear Diary,
>   Yesterday, I went to a
> fortune teller. She told me I
> was destined for

VI.   CONVERSATION ACTIVITIES

A.   Act It Out

DIRECTIONS: Read each of the following situations and act it out. Use as many idioms as possible. Work with a partner.

be destined for	make an impression on
get off to a good start	make use of
keep on	plan on
make a name for oneself	take an interest in

1. Your best friend is unhappy at work. He or she is thinking about changing fields. Discuss the situation. For example, say, "I don't think I'm destined for a career in . . ."

2. You've been working for the same company for ten years. Your boss just gave you an unsatisfactory annual evaluation. You think your performance has been excellent. Discuss it with your boss.

3. You are the parent of a very artistic boy who is finishing high school. Discuss his abilities and his future with his teacher.

B.   Talk It Over

1. Move around the room and find a classmate who . . .

   Write his or her name here.

   a. got off to a good start in his or her career. _____

   b. keeps on writing letters to a pen pal from childhood. _____

   c. hopes to make a name for himself or herself in the business world. _____

      How? _____

   d. never took an interest in sports. _____

   e. makes use of his or her time very well. _____

   f. is not planning on getting married. _____

   g. recently met someone who made an impression on him or her. _____

      Who was it? _____

   h. is destined for a happy life. _____

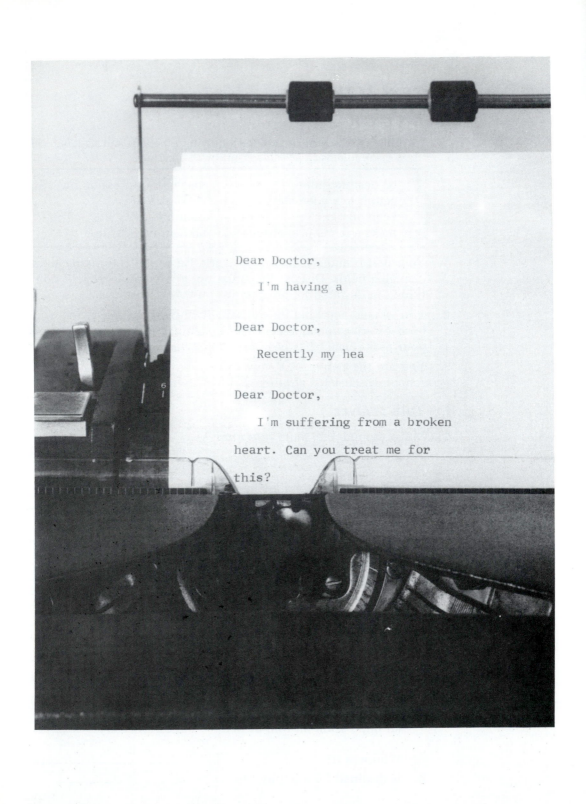

Dear Doctor,

    I'm having a

Dear Doctor,

    Recently my hea

Dear Doctor,

    I'm suffering from a broken

heart. Can you treat me for

this?

9 SICKNESS

WARM-UP EXERCISE

Many people have medical problems — for example, allergies, back pain, headaches, stomach aches. Do you have a medical problem, even a small one? Write your problem here.

_____

Tell your group about your medical problem and ask for advice on how to feel better. Write the advice here:

You should _____

_____

You shouldn't _____

_____

Do you think this is good advice for you?   ( ) yes   ( ) no

Why? _____

READING SELECTION

DIRECTIONS: Read the following story silently. Then do the reading exercises that follow.

Fight It Off

In the fourteenth century, an epidemic[1] of bubonic plague, a terrible disease, killed 25 million people in Europe. When the epidemic **broke out,** people called it the "Black Death." It spread when fleas[2] carrying the disease **came in contact with** rats.[3] When the fleas bit the rats, the disease went into the rats' bloodstreams. When the rats died, the fleas spread the disease to humans. People who got the disease **threw up,** and parts of their bodies became swollen.[4]

In the twentieth century, an epidemic of another plague, called AIDS (acquired immune deficiency syndrome), broke out. Like bubonic plague, AIDS is spread through the bloodstream.

In healthy people, the immune system **protects** the body **from** disease. AIDS causes the immune system to **break down.** Without the help of the immune system, the AIDS victim **suffers from** one sickness after another, including unusual types of cancer[5] and pneumonia.[6]

In 1981, the first patient[7] was **treated for** AIDS. In the following years, thousands **died of** this twentieth-century plague.

1. The spreading of a contagious disese.
2. A small bloodsucking insect that jumps from place to place.
3. A long-tailed rodent that is larger than a mouse.
4. Bigger, increased in size.
5. Deadly tumors.
6. Disease of the lungs.
7. A sick person.

I. READING EXERCISES

A. Get the Picture? Comprehension

DIRECTIONS: These questions are based on the story you just read. Write "True" or "False" after each statement.

1. When many people suddenly got bubonic plague, it was called the "Black Death."   **True**

2. Bubonic plague spread from rats to fleas.   _____

3. Vomiting was not a symptom of plague.   _____

4. The immune system keeps the body healthy.   _____

5. When a person got AIDS, the immune system continued to work.   _____

6. A person with AIDS never got any sicknesses.   _____

7. The first time a patient got medical help for AIDS was in 1981.   _____

8. AIDS killed thousands.   _____

B. Get the Picture? Inferences

DIRECTIONS: An inference is something that is not stated directly, but is implied. Write "True" or "False" after each inference.

1. It isn't easy to stop the spread of a plague.   _____

2. Doctors quickly stopped the spread of AIDS.   _____

3. AIDS, like bubonic plague, is spread through any physical contact — for example, shaking hands.   _____

C.   Get the Picture? Main Idea

DIRECTIONS: Mark the one statement that represents the main idea of the story.

1. ( ) Bubonic plague killed many people in the fourteenth century.

2. ( ) Like bubonic plague in the fourteenth century, a terrible disease called AIDS killed many people in the twentieth century.

3. ( ) The immune system is very important to the body. It keeps the body healthy so the person doesn't get sick.

II.   MEANING EXERCISES

A.   Figure It Out

DIRECTIONS: Mark the meaning of the idiom underlined in each sentence.

1.   As soon as the flu <u>breaks out</u>, Joe gets it.

    a.   (x) begins suddenly
    b.   ( ) hurts seriously
    c.   ( ) sends him to the hospital

2.   Every winter Joe <u>suffers from</u> the flu.

    a.   ( ) hates
    b.   ( ) is doing something about
    c.   ( ) is sick because of

3.   Joe never gets headaches or <u>throws up</u>, but he always gets the flu.

    a.   ( ) becomes sick
    b.   ( ) goes to bed
    c.   ( ) vomits

4.   Sometimes Joe gets depressed because he feels like his health is <u>breaking down</u>.

    a.   ( ) improving, getting better
    b.   ( ) failing, getting worse
    c.   ( ) important

5. After two weeks of being sick, Joe is sure he's going to <u>die of</u> the flu.

         a. ( ) kill himself because of
         b. ( ) die because of
         c. ( ) continue to have

6. But Joe never goes to the doctor to be <u>treated for</u> the flu.

         a. ( ) asked about
         b. ( ) examined
         c. ( ) given medical help for

7. Joe is afraid he will <u>come in contact with</u> other sick people and get sicker.

         a. ( ) meet, come near
         b. ( ) talk to
         c. ( ) examine and help

8. Joe thinks he should <u>protect</u> himself <u>from</u> other medical problems.

         a. ( ) study
         b. ( ) take medicine for
         c. ( ) keep safe from

B. What Does It Go With?

DIRECTIONS: Two of the three choices after each sentence can be correctly used with the idiom. Mark the *two* correct answers.

1. When Harry was in the hospital, he came in contact with

                           _____ .

         a. (x) a patient with skin cancer
         b. (x) a famous doctor
         c. ( ) the operating room
         Hint: The object must be another person or a condition, not a place.

2. Paula ate and drank so much at the birthday party that

    _____ threw up on the way home.

    a. ( ) the food
    b. ( ) she
    c. ( ) the poor little girl
    Hint: The subject must be a person.

3. Last year, _____ broke out across the country.

    a. ( ) a terrible flu
    b. ( ) a strange disease
    c. ( ) a patient
    Hint: The subject must be a medical problem.

4. If you get a flu shot, it will protect you from

    _____ this winter.

    a. ( ) getting sick
    b. ( ) the flu
    c. ( ) an injection
    Hint: The object must be a medical problem.

5. He was hospitalized because his _____ broke down.

    a. ( ) body
    b. ( ) immune system
    c. ( ) digestive system
    Hint: The subject must be a specific system in the body.

6. Victor isn't feeling well because he suffers from

    _____ .

    a. ( ) allergies
    b. ( ) a little cut on his hand
    c. ( ) arthritis
    Hint: The object must be a medical problem that continues.

7. Donna went to the doctor because of a bad sunburn, but she had

   to be treated for _____.

         a.   (   )   skin cancer
         b.   (   )   another skin problem
         c.   (   )   pills
         Hint: The object must be a medical problem.

8. If Andy isn't careful, he's going to die of _____.

         a.   (   )   his diet
         b.   (   )   a heart attack
         c.   (   )   pneumonia
         Hint: The object must be a medical problem.

C.   Look It Up

DIRECTIONS: Create your own minidictionary. For each idiom, write the *meaning*, an appropriate *subject*, a *direct object* or *object of the preposition* where indicated, and an *example sentence*. If you need help, refer to the other exercises in this section. Notice the stress (/) for each idiom, the position of the pronoun object [   ], and any special grammar or stylistic notes.

When you have created your minidictionary for each chapter, you can look an idiom up whenever you need to.

1. break out

   Meaning: **begin suddenly** _____

   Subject: **the flu** _____

   Example sentence: **The flu broke out this winter, and**

   everyone got it.

2. come in contact with [   ]

   Meaning: _____

   Subject: _____

   Object of preposition: _____

   Example sentence: _____

3. throw up
    Meaning: _____
    Subject: _____
    Example sentence: _____

4. protect [   ] from [   ]
    Meaning: _____
    Subject:
    Direct object: _____
    Object of preposition: _____
    Example sentence: _____

5. break down
    Meaning: _____
    Subject: _____
    Example sentence: _____

6. suffer from [   ]
    Meaning: _____
    Subject: _____
    Object of preposition: _____
    Example sentence: _____

7. treat [   ] for [   ]
    Meaning: _____
    Subject: _____
    Direct object: _____
    Object of preposition: _____
    Example sentence: _____

8. die of [   ]
    Meaning: _____
    Grammar note: the object is usually a noun
    Subject: _____
    Object of preposition: _____
    Example sentence: _____

III. GRAMMAR EXERCISES

A. Fill It In: Prepositions and Particles

> DIRECTIONS: Fill in the blanks with the correct prepositions or particles. Then play the tape and check your answers.

David was called the Bubble Boy. He suffered ____**from**____ a
₁
medical problem: His immune system didn't work. If the immune system doesn't work, the body is not protected _____ sickness.
₂

The doctors treated David _____ his disease by keeping
₃
him in a plastic bubble. That was the only way to be sure he didn't
come _____ contact _____ any sicknesses.
₄ ₅

The only hope for David was a bone-marrow transplant. This
would give him the cells he needed to protect his body
_____ disease. His older sister's bone marrow was trans-
₆
planted. There was finally hope of life outside the bubble for this
12-year-old boy. But after the operation, David got a fever and started
to throw _____.   His body's systems broke _____
₇ ₈
and the Bubble Boy died _____ his disease.
₉

B. Fill It In: Object Pronouns

> DIRECTIONS: In each sentence, fill in one of the blanks with the object pronoun in parentheses.

1. Stan didn't get the virus because he didn't come in contact

_____ with ____**it**____. (it)
_a _b

2. The sun is dangerous. Use this cream to protect yourself

_____ from _____. (it)
      a   b

3. Denise's arthritis is very painful in bad weather. On rainy days

she really suffers _____ from _____. (it)
                            a   b

4. The doctors say Mary's type of cancer is not serious. She's go-

ing into the hospital to be treated _____ for
                                              a

_____. (it)
   b

5. In the United States, each year many people develop heart disease

and die _____ of _____. (it)
                a   b

IV. LISTENING COMPREHENSION EXERCISE

A. Listen In

DIRECTIONS: You will hear a situation presented in one or two sentences. Listen to each situation and mark the response here that most closely corresponds to the situation.

1. a. ( ) In the United States, cancer kills more people than heart disease.

    b. (x) There are more deaths because of heart disease than any other illness in the United States.

    c. ( ) People don't die of heart disease in the United States any more.

2. a. ( ) Margie needs medication to keep her respiratory system working.

    b. ( ) Margie's respiratory system works fine.

    c. ( ) Margie doesn't need medication.

3. a. ( ) The effects of arthritis include back pain and stiff knees.

    b. ( ) Heart damage is the only effect of arthritis.

    c. ( ) People with arthritis don't have pain.

4. a. ( ) Rock Hudson, the movie actor, went to France for a visit.

    b. ( ) Rock Hudson went to France for medical help before he died of AIDS.

    c. ( ) Rock Hudson went to France to see AIDS victims.

5. a. ( ) The teenager's parents wanted to get the sleeping pills out of her stomach.

    b. ( ) The teenager vomited because the sleeping pills made her sick.

    c. ( ) The teenager's parents got sick.

6. a. ( ) The parents wanted children with AIDS to go to school.

    b. ( ) The parents were afraid their children would get AIDS if they were in school with an AIDS victim.

    c. ( ) The parents didn't think it was a problem if their children were in school with a child who had AIDS.

7. a. ( ) Very few people got the flu this winter.

    b. ( ) All the people in the office got the flu this winter.

    c. ( ) Everyone broke something in the office this winter.

8. a. ( ) People who go in the sun should not use sunscreen.

    b. ( ) The sun's rays are harmful, so the American Cancer Society recommends using sunscreen.

    c. ( ) If you use sunscreen, you will get cancer.

V. WRITING EXERCISE

A.   Finish It Up

DIRECTIONS: Finish this entry in your diary. Use as many idioms as you can.

Dear Diary,
    Yesterday, I saw an old
friend who suffers from

VI. CONVERSATION ACTIVITIES

A. Act It Out

> DIRECTIONS: Read each of the following situations and act it out. Use as many idioms as possible. Work with a partner.

1. A child got a deadly disease through a blood transfusion.[8] He is in your son's class in elementary school. You're attending a parents' meeting that was called to discuss the problem. Should the sick child be allowed to attend school? Discuss the situation with the other parents. For example, say, "Of course, we want to protect our children from disease . . ."

2. A member of your family is dying. She doesn't want her doctors to keep her alive with the help of machines. She feels she has the right to die. Discuss the situation with other family members.

3. One of your close friends thinks his nose is too big, and he wants to have plastic surgery to make it smaller. Discuss some of the reasons he should or shouldn't have the operation.

B. Talk It Over

Move around the room and find a classmate who . . .   Write his or her name here.

a. comes in contact with people with serious sicknesses. _____

b. has thrown up from drinking too much. _____

c. always protects himself or herself from the sun. _____

    How? _____

d. suffers from allergies. _____

e. has been treated for back pain. _____

f. has a relative who died of a heart attack. _____

g. was in school when an illness broke out and everybody got it. _____

    Which illness? _____

8. The transfer of blood from one person to another.

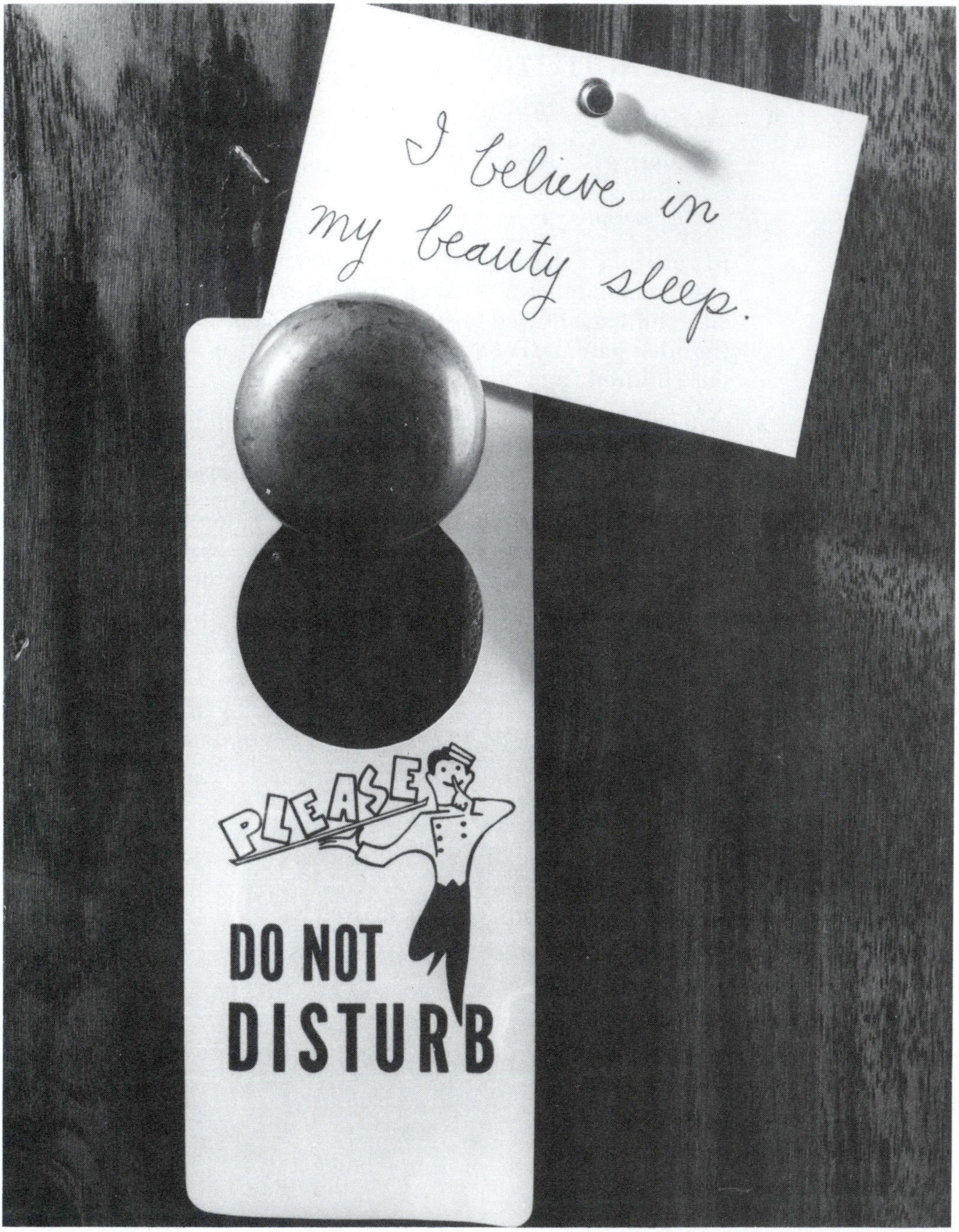
I believe in
my beauty sleep.
PLEASE
DO NOT
DISTURB

10 LIFESTYLES

WARM-UP EXERCISE

What is the one thing in your home that is more important to you than any other object?

_____

Arrange the following areas with the one most important to you first and the least important to you last.

Number _____: work

Number _____: school

Number _____: entertainment

Which one of these is more important to you?

Number _____: family

Number _____: friends

Share your answers with your group.

READING SELECTION

> DIRECTIONS: Read the following story silently. Then do the reading exercises that follow.

Live It Up

In the late 1960s and early 1970s, hippies **were wrapped up in** demonstrations[1] and drugs. Many hippies (or flower children, as they were called) left the cities to plant gardens in the country. The only clothes they wore were jeans and T-shirts. Hippies didn't want money or power; peace and love were all they **believed in.**

What **became of** the hippies? In the 1980s, many of them **turned into** yuppies (young, urban professionals). Yuppies loved big cities, where they changed old neighborhoods[2] into fashionable sections.

Looking good was important, so yuppies **worked out** in a health club, and spent a lot of money on their hair and clothes. After buying everything they needed to cook at home, they **ate out** most of the time. Yuppies really **lived it up.**

If looking good was important to yuppies, being successful at work was *very* important. Yuppies **were devoted to** making money. Many worked and **had** careers **on the side.** This extra business was often real estate.[3]

What's going to happen to the baby-boom generation[4] in the future? Some say they will develop another new lifestyle. Others say they will **settle down,** have children, and grow old, just like every other generation.

---

1. A public expression of opinion.
2. Areas, communities.
3. Land and the buildings on it.
4. People born between 1946 and 1964, when there was an unusually high birthrate in the United States.

I. READING EXERCISES

A. Get the Picture? Comprehension

DIRECTIONS: These questions are based on the story you just read. Write "True" or "False" after each statement.

1. Drugs were not important to hippies.   **False**

2. Peace and love were important to hippies.   _____

3. Nobody knows what happened to the hippies.   _____

4. Many hippies became yuppies in the 1980s.   _____

5. Yuppies are too busy to do exercise.   _____

6. Yuppies like to eat in restaurants.   _____

7. Yuppies live simple lives.   _____

8. Making money is not very important to yuppies.   _____

9. In addition to their regular jobs, many yuppies also have private businesses to help them make extra money.   _____

10. Some people say yuppies will get married, stay in one place, and grow old.   _____

B. Get the Picture? Inferences

DIRECTIONS: An inference is something that is not stated directly, but is implied. Write "True" or "False" after each inference.

1. What was important to people in the United States didn't change very much between the 1960s and the 1980s.   _____

2. Some people think the baby-boom generation is very changeable.   _____

C. Get the Picture? Main Idea

DIRECTIONS: Mark the one statement that represents the main idea of the story.

1. ( ) Peace and love were important to hippies, but clothes, money, and power weren't. Hippies preferred to live in the country, where they could grow their own vegetables.

2. ( ) The baby-boom generation has gone from being hippies, who didn't care about money and success, to being yuppies, who care a lot about money and success. What this generation will do next, nobody knows.

3. ( ) Yuppies want to look good and make a lot of money.

II. MEANING EXERCISES

A. Figure It Out

DIRECTIONS: Mark the meaning of the idiom underlined in each sentence.

1. The United States is fighting a big drug problem. Many young people are wrapped up in drugs.

   a. ( ) like
   b. (x) are completely involved in
   c. ( ) are completely against

2. Every year, more and more young people seem to believe in drugs.

   a. ( ) take, use
   b. ( ) don't use
   c. ( ) think of as important or good

3. Adults are very worried about what is going to become of these teenagers.

   a. ( ) stop, prevent
   b. ( ) happen to
   c. ( ) help

4. Some people think the next generation is going to <u>turn into</u> a generation of drug addicts.

        a. ( ) become
        b. ( ) be against
        c. ( ) look like

5. The young people don't seem to understand the problem. They just want to <u>live it up</u>.

        a. ( ) take drugs
        b. ( ) live poorly
        c. ( ) enjoy life

6. They like to have fun, <u>eat out</u>, and get high.

        a. ( ) eat everything they can
        b. ( ) eat at home
        c. ( ) eat in a restaurant

7. The young people don't think about their health and they don't <u>work out</u>.

        a. ( ) have a job outside, such as gardening
        b. ( ) do exercise, usually in a gym
        c. ( ) play basketball or football

8. Some young people aren't happy about their lives. They don't want to <u>be devoted to</u> drugs.

        a. ( ) take
        b. ( ) sell
        c. ( ) consider very important

9. Some young people don't want to <u>have</u> illegal businesses <u>on the side</u> to support their drug addiction.

        a. ( ) buy
        b. ( ) work for
        c. ( ) have in addition to a regular job

10. Instead they hope to <u>settle down</u> some day and live normal lives without drugs.

      a. ( ) stop taking drugs
      b. ( ) look for a job
      c. ( ) have a home and family

B. What Does It Go With?

DIRECTIONS: Two of the three choices after each sentence can be correctly used with the idiom. Mark the *two* correct answers.

1. Dave is really wrapped up in _____.

      a. (x) his homework
      b. (x) his religion
      c. ( ) the paper towels
    Hint: The object must be something important in one's life.

2. Dennis doesn't believe in _____.

      a. ( ) drinking while driving
      b. ( ) music
      c. ( ) using any kind of drugs
    Hint: The object must be something controversial.

3. What's going to become of _____ if she dies?

      a. ( ) her hospital bed
      b. ( ) her children
      c. ( ) her business
    Hint: The object must be someone or something that can change.

4. Everyone is very happy to see that Joan is turning into

_____.

      a. ( ) a fine musician
      b. ( ) a responsible woman
      c. ( ) the same person she always was
    Hint: The object must be someone or something that can change.

5. Every day at 5:30, ————————————— works out.

    a. ( ) Elaine
    b. ( ) the sick patient
    c. ( ) the boxing team
    Hint: The subject must be a person who can do exercise.

6. ————————————— eats out three times a week.

    a. ( ) Judy
    b. ( ) The whole family
    c. ( ) Their dog
    Hint: The subject must be a person.

7. ————————————— is going to live it up tonight.

    a. ( ) The director of the "Best Movie of the Year"
    b. ( ) The winner of the lottery
    c. ( ) The bottle of champagne
    Hint: The subject must be a person.

8. ————————————— is really devoted to his family.

    a. ( ) Bob's father
    b. ( ) Bob
    c. ( ) Hard work
    Hint: The subject must be a person.

9. Kevin has ————————————— on the side.

    a. ( ) a photography business
    b. ( ) his regular job
    c. ( ) a girlfriend
    Hint: The object must be someone or something extra.

10. ————————————— are going to settle down in Texas.

    a. ( ) Joseph and Patricia
    b. ( ) Mary's 5-year-old sons
    c. ( ) Barbara and her new husband
    Hint: The subject is usually an adult.

C. Look It Up

DIRECTIONS: Create your own minidictionary. For each idiom, write the *meaning*, an appropriate *subject*, a *direct object* or *object of the preposition* where indicated, and an *example sentence*. If you need help, refer to the other exercises in this section. Notice the stress (/) for each idiom, the position of the pronoun object [ ], and any special grammar or stylistic notes.

When you have created your minidictionary for each chapter, you can look an idiom up whenever you need to.

1. be wrapped up in [ ]
        Meaning: __be very involved in something__
        Subject: __graduate students__
        Object of preposition: __their courses__
        Example sentence: __Graduate students are so wrapped up in their courses that they don't have time to have fun.__

2. believe in [ ]
        Meaning: _____
        Subject: _____
        Object of preposition: _____
        Example sentence: _____

3. become of [ ]
        Meaning: _____
        Subject: _____
        Object of preposition: _____
        Example sentence: _____

4. turn into [ ]
        Meaning: _____
        Grammar note: __the object is usually a noun__
        Subject: _____
        Object of preposition: _____
        Example sentence: _____

5. work out
    Meaning: _____
    Stylistic note: __informal_____
    Subject: _____
    Example sentence: _____

6. eat out
    Meaning: _____
    Subject: _____
    Example sentence: _____

7. live [it] up
    Meaning: _____
    Grammar note: __the object is always "it"__
    Stylistic note: __informal_____
    Subject: _____
    Direct object: _____
    Example sentence: _____

8. be devoted to [   ]
    Meaning: _____
    Subject: _____
    Object of preposition: _____
    Example sentence: _____

9. have [   ] on the side
    Meaning: _____
    Grammar note: __the object is usually a noun__
    Subject: _____
    Direct object: _____
    Example sentence: _____

10. settle down
    Meaning: _____
    Subject: _____
    Example sentence: _____

III.   GRAMMAR EXERCISES

A.   Fill It In: Prepositions and Particles

DIRECTIONS: Fill in the blanks with the correct prepositions or particles. Then play the tape and check your answers.

William has no time for anybody. He's wrapped ____**up**____
₁

_____ his job. All he believes _____ is making
₂   ₃

money.

When he finished high school, he had a 50-hour-a-week job and

he had a business _____ the side selling T-shirts in the park
₄

on Sundays. In six months he had turned _____ a worka-
₅

holic (a person addicted to work). He made a lot of money but had no

time to eat _____ or live it _____ in other ways.
₆   ₇

If you ask him if he works _____, he says, "I don't work out,
₈

I just work!"

What's going to become _____ William in the future?
₉

He'll be a tired, lonely, but very rich man some day.

B.   Fill It In: Object Pronouns

DIRECTIONS: In each sentence, fill in *one* of the blanks with the object pronoun in parentheses.

1.   All she talks about is her new company. She's really wrapped

_____ up in ____**it**____. (it)
_a   _b

2. Ellen never drinks. She doesn't believe _____ in
   _a

   _____. (it)
   _b

3. Poor Frank. He became a drug addict at 14 and left school at 15.

   What's going to become _____ of _____?
   (him)   _a   _b

4. When Corinne inherited $50,000 after her grandmother died, she

   lived _____ up _____ (it) for many months.
         _a   _b

5. Albert loves his wife and children very much. He's really devoted

   _____ to _____. (them)
   _a   _b

IV. LISTENING COMPREHENSION EXERCISE

A. Listen In

DIRECTIONS: You will hear a situation presented in one or two sentences. Listen to each situation and mark the response here that most closely corresponds to the situation.

1. a. ( ) Tommy works after class every day.
   b. (x) Tommy can exercise in the gym at school every day.
   c. ( ) Tommy is lucky because he doesn't have to work after school.

2. a. ( ) Gary thinks people should work hard.
   b. ( ) Laura thinks people should work hard.
   c. ( ) Gary and Laura have the same ideas about life.

3. a. ( ) Claude works only as a stock broker.
   b. ( ) Claude has a full-time job as a stock broker and a part-time job in the music business.
   c. ( ) Claude isn't a yuppie.

4. a. ( ) Andy is still a young boy.

    b. ( ) Andy has no time for his mother.

    c. ( ) Andy gives a lot of attention to his mother.

5. a. ( ) Don became handsome as he got older.

    b. ( ) Don has a funny child.

    c. ( ) Don is a funny-looking child.

6. a. ( ) Everybody knows where Carol is and what she's doing.

    b. ( ) Nobody knows Carol.

    c. ( ) Nobody knows what happened to Carol after college.

7. a. ( ) Sandra is going to spend her next paycheck and have some fun.

    b. ( ) Sandra is going to save her next paycheck.

    c. ( ) Sandra lives upstairs.

8. a. ( ) Nina is married and lives a traditional life.

    b. ( ) Nina's mother wants her daughter to get married, have children, and live a traditional life.

    c. ( ) Nina lives like everybody else.

9. a. ( ) Andrea wasn't serious about the hippie movement.

    b. ( ) First, Andrea was involved in the women's movement and then, in the hippie movement.

    c. ( ) Andrea gets very involved in things like the hippie movement and the women's movement.

10. a. ( ) Robert loves Helen.

    b. ( ) Robert and Helen like to eat in restaurants.

    c. ( ) Robert and Helen don't like to eat in restaurants.

V. WRITING EXERCISE

A. Finish It Up

DIRECTIONS: Finish this entry in your diary. Use as many idioms as you can.

Dear Diary,
    I don't know what to do.
My best friend is turning into

VI. CONVERSATION ACTIVITIES

A. Act It Out

DIRECTIONS: Read each of the following situations and act it out. Use as many idioms as possible. Work with a partner.

become of	be wrapped up in	settle down
be devoted to	eat out	turn into
believe in	have on the side	work out
	live it up	

a. You are having personal problems and your best friend is too busy to help you. Discuss this situation. For example, say, "You're so wrapped up in your job that you don't have time . . ."

b. Describe yourself as you were ten years ago. What were you doing? What was important to you? Do you feel the same way now or have you changed? Tell this to your psychiatrist.

B. Talk It Over

Move around the room and find a class-mate who . . .   Write his or her name here.

a. is wrapped up in politics. _____

b. believes in astrology. _____

c. knows what became of his or her best friend from childhood. _____

   What? _____

d. turned into a workaholic. _____

e. works out regularly. _____

f. lives it up whenever he or she has the money. _____

g. is devoted to his or her family. _____

h. has a business on the side.

   What is it? _____

i. doesn't think he or she will ever settle down. _____

j. hates to eat out. _____

REVIEW II: WHAT'S UP?

WARM-UP EXERCISE

You're finishing this book, and perhaps you're finishing a course, too. You have probably had some positive experiences in the class. This is a chance to express what was positive for you. Complete these sentences and read them to the class:

The best thing that happened to me in this class was

_____.

In the future, when I think about this class, I'll remember

_____.

I. MIX THEM UP

DIRECTIONS: Mark the answer that completes each sentence correctly.

1. Every time I call Ken, he _____.

      a. (   ) is good at it
      b. (**x**) is on the phone
      c. (   ) is obsessed with it

2. Nobody was surprised that Richard went to Harvard University. He had gone to the best preschool, the best elementary school, and the best high school. He really _____.

      a. (   ) got in touch
      b. (   ) got through to it
      c. (   ) got off to a good start

3. If you want to learn how to play the piano, you can't just take lessons and practice for a few weeks. You have to

   _____ .

   a. ( ) keep it up
   b. ( ) keep in touch
   c. ( ) keep up with it

4. At the sales meeting, the new manager's speech was so good, he

   really _____ the whole department.

   a. ( ) made use of
   b. ( ) made a name for himself
   c. ( ) made an impression on

5. The vice president is going to leave the company soon, and the

   associate vice president is going to _____ .

   a. ( ) take care of it
   b. ( ) take over
   c. ( ) take in

II. TALK IT OVER

In almost every chapter you learned something about your class-mates by asking them questions. Now, choose one person and write a story about him or her, using the information from several chapters. As you write, you may need to get some more information from that person. Also, give your story a title. Here is an example.

Destined for Lincoln Center

Roger is good at playing the piano. (*from Chapter 1*) In fact, he grew up in a musical family. (*from Chapter 2*) His mother was a pianist, and his father was a conductor. When he was in school, he played the piano and the violin, and he sang in the chorus. He really stood out. (*from Chapter 1*) . . .

_____

_____

_____

_____

_____

_____

III. LISTEN IN

DIRECTIONS: Listen to the tape and mark the sentences you hear. Listen for the prepositions, the particles, the stress, and/or the objects.

1. a. (x) It broke down.
   b. ( ) It broke out.

2. a. ( ) Please try to get in touch with him.
   b. ( ) Please try to get through to him.

3. a. ( ) You have to keep on studying.
   b. ( ) You have to keep it up.

4. a. ( ) He's going to make an impression on them.
   b. ( ) He's going to make use of it.

5. a. ( ) That boxer doesn't stand out.
   b. ( ) That boxer doesn't stand a chance.

6. a. ( ) I'm sure you'll take an interest in it.
   b. ( ) I'm sure you'll take care of it.

7. a. ( ) What did you say he turned into?

    b. ( ) What did you say he turned down?

8. a. ( ) He knows he can't lose weight unless he works on it.

    b. ( ) He knows he can't lose weight unless he works out.

9. a. ( ) We don't know what she's against.

    b. ( ) We don't know what she's up against.

10. a. ( ) How much does she take in?

    b. ( ) How much does she take over?

IV. WHAT FOR?

In this book, you have studied the following idioms with the preposition "for":

be destined for
go for
make a name for oneself
pave the way for
root for
run for
√sign up for
treat for
vote for

DIRECTIONS: Rewrite each of the following sentences using an idiom with "for."

1. Helen just registered for a cooking course.

    Helen just signed up for a cooking course.

2. Paul was given medical help for cancer.

3. By the time Bill was thirty, he had already become famous.

_____

4. Everybody thinks that runner is going to be in the Olympics some day.

_____

5. Who did you support in the presidential election?

_____

6. Sally Ride, the first female astronaut in the United States, made it easier for other women to become astronauts.

_____

7. What basketball team are you going to support tonight?

_____

8. Did you ever want to try to become mayor of your city?

_____

9. Ryan thinks he's ready for the school soccer team. This year he's going to try to get on the team.

_____

V. WHAT'S UP?

Here is a list of idioms with the preposition "up" that you have learned in this book:

be up against	grow up
be wrapped up in	hang up
√bring up	keep up with
call up	sign up for
give up	throw up

DIRECTIONS: Rewrite the following story using as many of the idioms listed on page 159 as possible.

Betty lived in a small town when she was young. When she was about ten, she started to have trouble in school. She couldn't learn as fast as the other children. After spending hours trying to do her homework, she would stop trying. It was impossible for her. She would get so upset about her homework that she would become sick.

Sometimes she would telephone a classmate for help; but after trying to help Betty, they would get tired and end the conversation. Betty had a problem that millions of other people have: illiteracy.

Finally, her parents found a special literacy program for her, and she registered for literacy training. When she became an adult, she worked as a literacy volunteer, and was very involved in the literacy movement.

Betty was brought up in a small town.

_____

_____

_____

_____

_____

_____

_____

_____

VI. LOOK INTO THE FUTURE

DIRECTIONS: You're going to write messages for fortune cookies. Cut or tear up a piece of paper and write two fortunes using idioms you've learned. Write something positive! Put all the fortunes in a pile and have each member of the class choose two. If you wish, read the fortunes out loud to the class.

Examples:

> Soon you will come in contact with a person
> who will influence your life.

> The next time you are treated for a medical problem,
> you will fall in love with your doctor.

> Being single is fun,
> but it's time to settle down.

Across

3. She _____ the way for other female judges.
5. He can't _____ out the math problem.
8. The doctors said his respiratory system _____ down.
9. Every style that fashion designer creates _____ on.
10. That nurse comes in _____ with very sick patients.
14. Charles never took an _____ in his children.
17. When are you going to _____ down?
18. To eat quickly means to _____ off
20. Her parents _____ of all her boyfriends.
22. To continue means to _____ it up
24. She is _____ to her husband and children.
26. On New Year's Day, the President will be _____ in.
27. _____ on one thing at a time.
28. A fortune teller told him he's _____ for financial success.
29. To register for a course means to _____ up for a course
30. She is _____ against the best swimmers in the world.

Down

1. Can you do _____ sugar in your coffee?
2. You should keep in _____ with your friends.
3. The Democrats were put into _____.
4. To stop attending means to _____ out
6. To telephone means to call ___
7. Bob is _____ up in his own problems.
11. He's being _____ for cancer.
12. She just gave _____ to a baby boy.
13. Do you believe ___ astrology?
15. He has always _____ from back pain.
16. Billy doesn't _____ in drugs.
19. Doris was _____ up in Florida.
21. The boxing champion, Joe Lewis, made an _____ on the young boxer.
23. Americans are _____ with dieting.
25. After many years, he is _____ an interest in his family.

APPENDICES

APPENDIX A: LIST OF PREPOSITIONS AND PARTICLES

Prepositions

against	of
at	on
for	to
from	with
in	without
into	

Particles

apart	out
down	over
in	through
off	up

APPENDIX B: IDIOMS LISTED ACCORDING TO PREPOSITIONS AND PARTICLES

against
be against
compete against
be up against

apart
tell apart

at
be good at

down
break down
gulp down
settle down
turn down

for
be destined for
go for
make a name for oneself
pave the way for
root for
run for
sign up for
treat for
vote for

from
protect from
suffer from

in
believe in
be wrapped up in
come in contact with
get in touch with
keep in touch with
swear in
take an interest in
take in

into
put into power

of
become of
die of
disapprove of
drop out of
make use of
stand a chance of
take care of

off
get off to a good start
polish off
pull off

on
be on the phone
catch on

focus on
have on the side
keep on
make an impression on
plan on
work on

out
break out
drop out of
eat out
figure out
fill out
stand out
win out
work out

over
take over
tide over

to
be devoted to
get off to a good start
get through to
give birth to
stick to

through
get through to

up
be up against
be wrapped up in
bring up
call up
give up
grow up
hang up
keep up
keep up with

live it up
sign up for
throw up

with
be obsessed with
come in contact with
get in touch with
keep in touch with
keep up with
mix with

without
do without

APPENDIX C: IDIOMS LISTED ALPHABETICALLY BY VERB

be against
be destined for
be devoted to
be good at
be obsessed with
be on the phone
be up against
be wrapped up in
become of
believe in
break down
break out
bring up

call up
catch on
come in contact with
compete against

die of
disapprove of
do without
drop out of

eat out

figure out
fill out
focus on

get in touch with
get off to a good start
get through to
give birth to
give up
go for
grow up
gulp down

hang up
have on the side

keep in touch with
keep on
keep up
keep up with

live it up

make a name for oneself
make an impression on
make use of
mix with

pave the way for
plan on
polish off
protect from
pull off
put into power

root for
run for

settle down
sign up for
stand a chance of
stand out
stick to
suffer from
swear in

take an interest in

take care of
take in
take over
tell apart
throw up

tide over
treat for
turn down
turn into

vote for
win out
work on
work out

APPENDIX D: VERBS PLUS . . .

Verb + Particle

break down
break out
bring up
call up
catch on
eat out
figure out
fill out
give up

grow up
gulp down
hang up
keep up
live (it) up
polish off
pull off
settle down
stand out

swear in
take in
take over
tell apart
throw up
tide over
turn down
win out
work out

Verb + Particle + Preposition

be up against
drop out of
get through to

keep up with
sign up for

Verb + Preposition

be against
become of
believe in
compete against
die of
disapprove of
do without

focus on
go for
keep on
mix with
plan on
protect from
root for

run for
stick to
suffer from
treat for
turn into
vote for
work on

Complex Combinations Consisting of a Verb + Some of the Following: Particle, Preposition, Noun, Adjective

be destined for
be devoted to

be good at
be obsessed with

be on the phone
be wrapped up in

come in contact with
get in touch with
get off to a good start
give birth to
have on the side

keep in touch with
make a name for oneself
make an impression on
make use of
pave the way for

put into power
stand a chance of
take an interest in
take care of

APPENDIX E: VERB FORMS

Infinitive	Past	Past Participle
be	was, were	been
become	became	become
believe	believed	believed
break	broke	broken
bring	brought	brought
call	called	called
catch	caught	caught
come	came	come
compete	competed	competed
die	died	died
disapprove	disapproved	disapproved
do	did	done
drop	dropped	dropped
eat	ate	eaten
figure	figured	figured
fill	filled	filled
focus	focused	focused
get	got	gotten
give	gave	given
go	went	gone
grow	grew	grown
gulp	gulped	gulped
hang	hung	hung
have	had	had
keep	kept	kept
live	lived	lived
make	made	made
mix	mixed	mixed
pave	paved	paved
plan	planned	planned
polish	polished	polished
protect	protected	protected
pull	pulled	pulled
put	put	put
root	rooted	rooted

Infinitive	Past	Past Participle
run	ran	run
settle	settled	settled
sign	signed	signed
stand	stood	stood
stick	stuck	stuck
suffer	suffered	suffered
swear	swore	sworn
take	took	taken
tell	told	told
throw	threw	thrown
tide	tided	tided
treat	treated	treated
turn	turned	turned
vote	voted	voted
win	won	won
work	worked	worked

APPENDIX F: TAPE SCRIPTS

Chapter 1 — Sports

1. Terry isn't patriotic at all. He never roots for the American team.

2. Big Bob is definitely going to win the heavyweight boxing championship. He's competing against a boxer who's ten years older.

3. Elaine doesn't think she can win the piano competition this year, but she's going to go for it next year.

4. Many employees believed that some day Walter would become president of the company because he really stood out as a manager.

5. As a child, Maria liked to make speeches. Her parents knew she'd be good at politics when she got older.

Chapter 2 — Family

1. Barbara and Paul are always fighting, because Paul doesn't want Barbara to work. He thinks she should stay home and take care of their 3-year-old daughter, but Barbara wants to get a babysitter.

2. Frank was born in Chicago, but he was brought up in London. That's why he speaks English with a British accent.

3. Diane's doctor told her she's going to give birth to twins.

4. The only way to tell Michael and James apart is the birthmark Michael has near his left eye.

5. Nancy was born in Massachusetts, but her father was in the army, so she grew up on a military base in Texas.

Chapter 3 — Communication

1. Last night Joe's wife had a heart attack at home. Joe called the police emergency number, but he couldn't get through. His wife died.

2. If you want to have good friends, you have to keep in touch with them.

3. When Bruno first came to the United States from Italy, he was so nervous about his English that he never called anyone up. He preferred to talk in person.

4. A lot of people just hang up the phone when they hear Susan's answering machine.

5. Janet wants to get in touch with her favorite writer, but she doesn't know how.

6. Doug and Doris had a fight because Doug wanted to talk to Doris, but she was on the phone all night.

Chapter 4 — Education

1. Kevin wasn't considered for the job because he never finished filling out the application form.

2. Elizabeth won $10.00 in school today because she was the first one to figure out the solution to the math problem.

3. If Timothy is going to play that piano concerto in the concert next week, he had better keep working on it.

4. Donna has been so upset about her husband's health that she can't focus on her work or her children.

5. In many areas, senior citizens who can't leave their houses can sign up for Meals on Wheels. Their food will be delivered to their homes every day.

6. Carl dropped out of college in his second year, but he went back many years later and got a Bachelor's and a Master's degree.

7. Robert walks so fast that no one can keep up with him.

Chapter 5 — Food

1. Don's doctor recommended carrots and celery to tide him over between meals.

2. Many doctors recommend that their patients either do without egg yolks completely or eat only two or three a week.

3. Quick weight-loss programs usually don't work. You need a diet and exercise plan that you can stick to forever.

4. If you gulp down your meals, you're probably still hungry when you finish. If you eat slower, you'll eat less.

5. To reduce stress, sit in a quiet, comfortable place, close your eyes, and relax your muscles from feet to head. Then take in one deep breath after another and let each one out slowly.

6. If you think cottage cheese is boring, mix it with plain, low-fat yogurt and add apples, raisins, and a few walnuts.

7. Linda is obsessed with exercise. She goes to the gym every morning before work and runs every night after work. All weekend she plays tennis. She doesn't have time for anything else.

8. Bob must have a drinking problem. He says he wants just one beer, and then he polishes off five or six cans.

Chapter 6 — Persistence

1. Charles started the race at a fast pace but he couldn't keep it up and he didn't reach the finish line.

2. Songs from other countries don't usually catch on in the United States unless the words are in English.

3. Most of the professors say that Elaine stands a very good chance of getting a Ph.D.

4. Mark wanted to join the army after high school, but he was turned down for medical reasons.

5. Even though the hockey team hasn't won a game, they will never give up.

6. Pierre wants to stay in the United States, but his parents want him to return to France. He thinks he's going to win out.

7. David's coach told him he'd have to lose 30 pounds if he wanted to be in the Olympics. It wasn't easy but David pulled it off.

8. When Jennifer was a high school student in a small town, it was easy to be the best in the class. Now that she's at Harvard University, she's up against some of the smartest students in the country.

Chapter 7 — Politics

1. Nelson Rockefeller was sworn in as governor of New York four times.

2. According to the latest poll, most Americans disapprove of the way the President is doing his job.

3. The President's family doesn't want him to run for another term in office.

4. The whole state of Illinois voted for the Republican candidate because he was born in a small town in that state.

5. Many people think this is not a good time to put a new person into power.

6. When President Nixon left office, Vice President Ford took over.

7. The Senate seems to be against United States involvement in Central America and South America.

8. Peace talks may pave the way for peace in the Middle East.

Chapter 8 — Success

1. It isn't going to be easy for Doug to make a name for himself as a comedian.

2. George doesn't waste anything. He can make use of the smallest piece of paper.

3. When Lisa went to Japan, she took an interest in the Japanese language. When she returned to the States, she started studying it in college.

4. When Tom arrived for Thanksgiving dinner in old jeans and a dirty shirt, he didn't make a very good impression on his girlfriend's parents.

5. Carol had already lost $500 at the casino, but she kept on gambling.

6. Joan was destined for a career in the music world. Both of her parents were musicians.

7. Anne's photography project got off to a good start, but she never finished it because she didn't have enough money.

8. Jeff was planning on studying law, but he wasn't accepted by any law schools.

Chapter 9 — Sickness

1. In the United States, more people die of heart disease than any other disease. Cancer is the number two killer.

2. If Margie doesn't get her medication, her respiratory system will break down.

3. People who have arthritis suffer from back pain, swollen wrists, stiff knees, heart damage, and many other medical problems.

4. American movie star Rock Hudson went to France to be treated for AIDS, a disease that eventually killed him.

5. After the depressed teenager took a bottle of sleeping pills, her parents forced her to throw up. They then took her to the hospital.

6. In the 1980s, there were problems when some parents tried to stop children with AIDS from attending school. They didn't want their own children to come in contact with the deadly disease.

7. When the flu broke out this winter, everyone in the office got it.

8. The American Cancer Society recommends that people who must be in the sun use sunscreen to protect themselves from the sun's harmful rays.

Chapter 10 — Lifestyles

1. Tommy is lucky. Because his school has a great gym, he can work out after class every day.

2. Gary and his sister, Laura, are very different. Gary believes in working hard, and Laura believes in having fun.

3. Claude is a typical yuppie. He is a stock broker, and he has a music business on the side.

4. Everyone calls Andy a "Mama's boy" because he's completely devoted to his mother.

5. Don was a funny-looking child, but he turned into a very handsome man.

6. Nobody knows what became of Carol. After college, she disappeared.

7. Sandra has been saving money, but when she gets her next paycheck, she's really going to live it up.

8. Nina's mother can't understand why her daughter can't settle down like everybody else.

9. First, Andrea was wrapped up in the hippie movement for ten years. Then, she got involved in the women's liberation movement.

10. Robert and Helen love to eat out. Every week they try a new restaurant.

Review II

1. It broke down.

2. Please try to get through to him.

3. You have to keep on studying.

4. He's going to make use of it.

5. That boxer doesn't stand a chance.

6. I'm sure you'll take care of it.

7. What did you say he turned down?

8. He knows he can't lose weight unless he works out.

9. We don't know what she's up against.

10. How much does she take over?

ANSWER KEY

1. SPORTS

I. **A:** 1. True; 2. False; 3. False; 4. True; 5. True. **B:** 1. True; 2. True; 3. True. **C:** 1.

II. **A:** 1. c; 2. a; 3. b; 4. b; 5. c. **B:** 1. a & b; 2. b & c; 3. b & c; 4. a & c; 5. a & b.

III. **A:** 1. at; 2. out; 3. for; 4. against; 5. for. **B:** 1. b; 2. b; 3. b; 4. b.

IV. **A:** 1. b; 2. c; 3. c; 4. a; 5. b.

2. FAMILY

I. **A:** 1. True; 2. True; 3. False; 4. False; 5. False. **B:** 1. True; 2. False; 3. True. **C:** 3.

II. **A:** 1. b; 2. a; 3. c; 4. a; 5. c. **B:** 1. b & c; 2. a & c; 3. b & c; 4. b & c; 5. a & b.

III. **A:** 1. to; 2. apart; 3. of; 4. up; 5. up. **B:** 1. b; 2. a; 3. b; 4. a.

IV. **A:** 1. c; 2. a; 3. c; 4. a; 5. b.

3. COMMUNICATION

I. **A:** 1. True; 2. False; 3. True; 4. True. **B:** 1. True; 2. False; 3. True. **C:** 2.

II. **A:** 1. b; 2. b; 3. a; 4. a; 5. c; 6. c. **B:** 1. a & c; 2. a & b; 3. a & c; 4. b & c; 5. a & b; 6. b & c.

III. **A:** 1. in; 2. with; 3. up; 4. up; 5. in; 6. with. **B:** 1. a; 2. b; 3. a; 4. b.

IV. **A:** 1. b; 2. a; 3. b; 4. c; 5. b; 6. c.

4. EDUCATION

I. **A:** 1. False; 2. True; 3. True; 4. True; 5. False; 6. True; 7. False. **B:** 1. False; 2. True; 3. True. **C:** 2.

II. **A:** 1. c; 2. a; 3. b; 4. c; 5. b; 6. b; 7. c. **B:** 1. a & c; 2. a & b; 3. b & c; 4. a & b; 5. b & c; 6. a & b; 7. b & c.

III. **A:** 1. up; 2. for; 3. out; 4. on; 5. out; 6. on; 7. out; 8. of; 9. up; 10. with. **B:** 1. a; 2. a; 3. b; 4. b; 5. b; 6. b.

IV. **A:** 1. b; 2. a; 3. b; 4. b; 5. c; 6. a; 7. c.

5. FOOD

I. **A:** 1. True; 2. True; 3. False; 4. True; 5. False; 6. False; 7. True; 8. True.
B: 1. True; 2. True; 3. False. **C:** 2.

II. **A:** 1. a; 2. b; 3. a; 4. c; 5. a; 6. b; 7. c; 8. a. **B:** 1. a & b; 2. a & b;
3. a & c; 4. a & b; 5. a & c; 6. a & b; 7. a & b; 8. b & c.

III. **A:** 1. down; 2. off; 3. with; 4. over; 5. in; 6. with; 7. without; 8. to.
C: 1. a; 2. a; 3. b; 4. a; 5. b; 6. b; 7. b.

IV. **A:** 1. b; 2. c; 3. a; 4. c; 5. b; 6. c; 7. c; 8. b.

VI. **C:** 1. f or g; 2. c; 3. b; 4. h; 5. a; 6. g or f; 7. e; 8. d.

REVIEW I

I. 1. c; 2. f; 3. e; 4. h; 5. d; 6. b; 7. g; 8. a; 9. i.

II. 1. b; 2. b; 3. a; 4. b.

III. 1. call; 2. hang; 3. grew; 4. bring; 5. sign; 6. keeping.

IV. 1. stood out; 2. filled out; 3. figure out; 4. dropped out.

V. 1. obsessed; 2. got; 3. keep; 4. mix; 5. do.

VI. 1. call up; 2. get in touch with; 3. get through; 4. hang up; 5. was on the phone;
5. gulped down; 7. polished off; 8. stick to; 9. figure out; 10. being obsessed
with; 11. keep in touch with.

VII.

Across clues		Down clues	
4. apart	13. working	1. keep	10. through
5. phone	14. do	2. stands	15. off
7. obsessed	16. hang	3. touch	17. gulp
9. birth	18. figure	6. tide	19. root
11. dropped	20. for	8. brought	
12. care			

6. PERSISTENCE

I. **A:** 1. True; 2. True; 3. True; 4. True; 5. False; 6. True; 7. False.
B: 1. True; 2. True; 3. True. **C:** 3.

II. **A:** 1. c; 2. a; 3. b; 4. c; 5. a; 6. b; 7. a; 8. c. **B:** 1. a & b; 2. a & b;
3. a & c; 4. b & c; 5. b & c; 6. a & b; 7. a & c; 8. a & c.

III. **A:** 1. of; 2. up; 3. up; 4. off; 5. up; 6. against; 7. out; 8. down.
B: 1. a; 2. a; 3. a.

IV. **A:** 1. b; 2. c; 3. b; 4. c; 5. a; 6. c; 7. a; 8. b.

176

7. POLITICS

I. **A:** 1. False; 2. True; 3. False; 4. True; 5. False; 6. True; 7. True; 8. False.
    B: 1. False; 2. False; 3. True. **C:** 1.

II. **A:** 1. c; 2. a; 3. c; 4. b; 5. a; 6. c; 7. a; 8. a. **B:** 1. b & c; 2. a & b;
    3. b & c; 4. a & b; 5. a & c; 6. a & b; 7. a & b; 8. a & b.

III. **A:** 1. for; 2. for; 3. into; 4. of; 5. over; 6. in. **B:** 1. b; 2. a; 3. b; 4. a;
    5. b; 6. b; 7. b.

IV. **A:** 1. a; 2. c; 3. c; 4. a; 5. a; 6. c; 7. a; 8. b.

8. SUCCESS

I. **A:** 1. True; 2. False; 3. True; 4. True; 5. False; 6. True; 7. True; 8. True.
    B: 1. False; 2. False; 3. True. **C:** 1.

II. **A:** 1. a; 2. c; 3. b; 4. a; 5. a; 6. b; 7. c; 8. a. **B:** 1. b & c; 2. b & c;
    3. a & b; 4. b & c; 5. b & c; 6. a & c; 7. b & c; 8. a & c.

III. **A:** 1. on; 2. of; 3. in; 4. on; 5. off; 6. to; 7. for. **B:** 1. b; 2. b; 3. b;
    4. b; 5. b; 6. b.

IV. **A:** 1. b; 2. a; 3. b; 4. b; 5. a; 6. b; 7. a; 8. c.

9. SICKNESS

I. **A:** 1. True; 2. False; 3. False; 4. True; 5. False; 6. False; 7. True; 8. True.
    B: 1. True; 2. False; 3. False. **C:** 2.

II. **A:** 1. c; 2. a; 3. c; 4. b; 5. b; 6. c; 7. a; 8. c. **B:** 1. a & b; 2. b & c;
    3. a & b; 4. a & b; 5. b & c; 6. a & c; 7. a & b; 8. b & c.

III. **A:** 1. from; 2. from; 3. for; 4. in; 5. with; 6. from; 7. up; 8. down; 9. of.
    B: 1. b; 2. b; 3. b; 4. b; 5. b.

IV. **A:** 1. b; 2. a; 3. a; 4. b; 5. a; 6. b; 7. b; 8. b.

10. LIFESTYLES

I. **A:** 1. False; 2. True; 3. False; 4. True; 5. False; 6. True; 7. False; 8. False;
    9. True; 10. True. **B:** 1. False; 2. True. **C:** 2.

II. **A:** 1. b; 2. c; 3. b; 4. a; 5. c; 6. c; 7. b; 8. c; 9. c; 10. c.
    B: 1. a & b; 2. a & c; 3. b & c; 4. a & b; 5. a & c; 6. a & b; 7. a & b;
    8. a & b; 9. a & c; 10. a & c.